a little bit of
angels

a little bit of
angels

an introduction to
spirit guidance

ELAINE CLAYTON

STERLING ETHOS
New York

STERLING ETHOS
New York

STERLING ETHOS and the distinctive Sterling Ethos logo are
registered trademarks of Sterling Publishing Co., Inc.

ISBN 978-1-4549-6070-6
ISBN 978-1-4549-2901-7 (e-book)

For information about custom editions, special sales, and premium
purchases, please contact specialsales@unionsquareandco.com.

Printed in India

2 4 6 8 10 9 7 5 3 1

unionsquareandco.com

Cover and interior design by Kaylie Pendleton

Cover image: nu kristle/Shutterstock.com
Interior Images: Getty Images: PeterHermesFurian/iStock/Getty Images Plus: 48;
Shutterstock.com: Aleksej015: vi; ByVector: viii; nu kristle: throughout (halo)

contents

INTRODUCTION

I cannot recall a time when I did not believe in angels. Certainly my conditioning in early childhood included an awareness of angels, for which I am grateful. Growing up with a sense of some kind of atmospheric "other," I was open to the presence of divine helpmates, even though they were remote or, for the most part, invisible. This orientation meant that I felt supported by an unseen legion or at least by one particular guardian. Even an ordinary day was experienced as surprising and delightful because the expectation of spiritual assistance was there. I saw synchronistic happenings as signs. For example, the wind blowing a door open for me at just the right moment was really an agent of the wind or an angel's hands aiding me. I reflect on the days of my life and see how I imagined the unseen not only within us but within the spaces between us, between each other and objects, to be filled with a force of love. It is that which I long to cultivate and share with others.

I have dreamed of, thought of, read about, and painted angels for most of my life. Angels and the realms they move through commingle with my 3-D reality as a natural part of me being me. I don't think I'd like a world empty of the notion or concept of spiritual guides. Those of us who have felt the existence of angels—and those who have yet to do so—continuously add to or detract from a collective consciousness about angels. If enough of us nurture knowledge of angels through our curiosity, sense of wonderment, and spiritual

longing to learn and grow, I believe goodness will prevail over whatever brings misery to our lives. If it is true that we have what we hold or that we get what we put out there, then, as creators in our own right, angels are with us. They exist simply because we discovered that there was something more going on than just what seems obvious on the surface, and they exist all the more because we wish them into actuality.

This book was written with a sincere intention to contribute to an age-old appreciation of angelic beings and as a gesture of respect for all of humanity—as we live and breathe, day by day, through current individual struggles and aspirations. I believe such struggles, whether ordinary or extreme and bizarre, are less difficult when we become objective. In our own experiences of whatever may be causing sorrow or fear, allowing impressions of the mysterious and impalpable to blend in as part of those experiences thoroughly alters our perception. Having an awareness of angels is to have a bird's-eye view, because angels are not us—they are watching us. This added dimension of "being watched" by invisible and benevolent forces most definitely opens our consciousness, deepening our awareness of our actions and reactions, as we ask "How is an angel viewing me right now?" or "How does an angel see this situation I'm in?" And as we aspire to express our unique personalities—fulfill our individual purposes—that angel's-eye view helps, because we begin to see that we are not trapped as subject to conditions; we create them, solve them, remove them, and at times cooperate with them. Our dreams come true as we mature when we disallow what harms us and welcome what brings us loving abundance.

Come along with me to look into the business of angels among us and connect to the enigmatic, mystical, and uncanny. I hope that by spending a little bit of time exploring the world of angels—which we'll do through playful expectation, journal writing, and dreaming—this book will encourage and inspire you to tune in to your very own angels. Asking and receiving angelic wisdom is joyous because doing so helps you engage with your own sense of wonder in such an expansive, positive way. *A Little Bit of Angels* was written in the spirit of honoring that invisible force of love and angelic passion that whirls within each of us and surrounds us evermore.

1

are there really such things as angels?

Before you read this book, close your eyes while you flip through it and then put your finger on one of the pages at random. Open your eyes. Did your finger land on a word? If so, write it down. Do this three times so you have three words. If you do it and your finger lands on a blank area, do it again until you have three words. This is one of the ways you can start a playful relationship with your angels and communicate in a joyous way with serendipity (an angel's cup of tea is made of serendipity!). Think about the words; notice them and the ways in which they may hold meaning for you. You can ask for answers to questions you may have and find three words as angel guidance to help solve problems. Play this angel game often with any book you like, but especially this book. And especially while having a cup of tea.

Don't you want to have and know an invisible friend who watches over you, steers you away from danger, and removes obstacles from your path? If you could summon angels—benevolent spiritual entities— that have your best interest as their main focus, wouldn't you want to call them to you? Would it matter whether or not any of us could *prove* that such holy entities exist, or would it simply be accepted as a wondrous and mysterious part of human life, worth having and exploring? Are angels a sweet bonus to counterbalance our common suffering?

Angels ARE real. And you've got one. In fact, you've got many. You have an angel for anything necessary, which means you've got different angels according to different phases and needs throughout your life. And not only that—you have within you as a natural-born creator the ability to even *create angels* according to your intentions and thought forms! Not bad, huh?

The human desire for spiritual helpers and guides and the inner sense that such presences are among us, albeit mostly invisible to us, is a universal inclination. We may feel utterly alone or desperate at times, especially during difficult situations. We not only long for relief or help, but we also inwardly desire it to the point that we ask for spiritual assistance readily, expectantly. The expectation that angelic help is there is the most important aspect to communing with angels. When we assert what we think we need and expect spiritual help, the universe cooperates. In time, the help we asked for arrives in a way that is evident to us, sometimes quickly but not always.

But what about the times when help does not seem to come after practically begging for it for a long while? Perhaps there is a spiritual lesson in endurance and patience at hand, and angels (in distress over our pain) are doing all kinds of things to help us but we are missing the obvious signs of that (see Chapter 10, page 85, for a list of common signs from your angels). In those cases when we feel that we struggle without help, we have to remember that, as creators, what we create becomes "real" in many ways, including the presence of angels in our lives.

Acknowledging that we are capable of generating energy and momentum toward our desires as we live and breathe is important and empowering. And we desire to be fulfilled, healthy, loved, and actualized in our talents and ideas. A conscious awareness of a mighty force of atmospheric advocates makes the life journey more interesting and exciting, don't you think? Angels don't necessarily need to be acknowledged by us to come through for us, but when we are consciously aware of them, life is more bountiful. This means we have to trust even the periods of time when we feel crushed or stuck or alone in our misery. Trust that you've asked for help and it *is* being spiritually dealt with, and breathe knowing—not just thinking but inwardly *knowing*—that angels exist. Watch and see. If believing in angels is a little strange for you, try it out of a sense of playfulness. If you're suffering greatly, you might not feel too playful, but when it comes to asking for divine intervention that you can't know even exists, what do you have to lose in assuming it does? And a child-like playful lightness of being is the best way to align with angelic mediation.

BELIEF OR EXPERIENTIAL?

Welcoming angels into our lives is one of the best parts of living. We humans are capable of receiving revelatory information, miraculous intervention, and superhuman strength without any explanation making sense other than "An angel helped me!" We can acknowledge that something supernatural is happening, or at least something that defies our sense of logic and understanding (such as an eight-year-old boy lifting a car off his father, or a person at the airport waiting to board a plane and getting a strong urge to take another flight instead, only to discover later that the plane they were supposed to be on had crashed after takeoff). To those who have been exposed to this feeling of being guided and helped by something ethereal or receiving a spiritual message, no validation from others that the angelic experience was "real" is necessary. This otherworldly support is so stunning and life-enhancing.

Experiencing that kind of benevolent, magical, unexplainable angelic event without knowing exactly how or why it unfolded as it did is complete, in and of itself. And upon reflection after the mysterious scenario unfolded, the telling of the angelic encounter lends food for life as it is recounted time and again. People touched by angels marvel at the way in which that divine intervention set them on a course that proved to be beneficial in a multitude of ways.

Those who have personally experienced that angelic brush of gold know within that something otherworldly took place and usually don't feel compelled to question it, yet they may ponder the puzzling aspects of these occurrences. This brings up some questions, such as in the example of the flight when that person had a strong feeling not to board the plane—what about the people who did board the flight and consequently died? Where were *their* angels? We won't know all the answers to life and death, even our own, but calling forth from God and His agents to help us and then following hunches and small urgings adds a lot of impressive meaning to our days.

QUESTIONS, QUESTIONS . . .

Pondering and questioning but not having to prove the existence of angels and the curious angelic events that we experience is a good thing. Always. Questioning is the best way to avoid a life of being tragically fooled by charlatans or evil dictators. In my own experience, I have found that angels are trying to help all of us have an inner dialogue about our own truths so they can guide us. *You've got to be listening inward to be aware of spiritual presence.* So centering the self and questioning if angels exist is good because it is you deciding for yourself. I sense that the angels themselves would prefer that we question their existence because it is our birthright to explore, discover, and learn on our own terms with our own free will. They see us experiencing our life struggles and questions and look upon us with mercy and mirth. Question each and every seemingly miraculous thing that unfolds in life! In doing so, I think what you'll find is that, even when there are rational or logical explanations of events, everything lines up to create the most beneficial situation possible, and that is a form of angelic intervention as well.

Skeptics, or even experts of one kind or another, might say that the little fifty-pound boy who saved his dad from under a one-and-a-half-ton car had a sudden burst of fear-induced adrenaline that temporarily altered his body's potential to achieve phenomenal, superhuman physical acts. Even if that is so, angels must at times, if not always, *use our laws of nature* here on Earth to accomplish their deeds. Gingerly or in the blink of an eye, they are able to play with our conditions of gravity and our reasoning skills as well as our sequential order of time. Whether defying earthbound scientific laws of nature or working through those same laws, happenstance and blithe providence is the predilection of angels for the benefit of humankind. Let it be known!

THE SCRUFFY RED-HEADED ANGEL

I recall being a passenger in a car that spun out, ending up backward and tilted in a ditch in the middle of nowhere on a lonely Georgia highway. The driver had been going too fast. Shaken and upset, getting out of the car and climbing out of the ditch, I was whispering prayers and noted to myself that during the spin I had calmly put my hand on the dashboard and put my head down. Why had I been so calm during a potentially very dangerous happening? Not even out of the ditch yet, I looked up and saw a tow truck approach and slow down. There was no other car anywhere as far as I could see, besides the one I just pulled myself out of, yet a tow truck showed up at the exact moment it was needed. I am sure I was gaping in astonishment as the tow-truck driver pulled off the highway a few feet from me and the driver of the ditched car.

A red-haired, bulky man stepped out of the tow truck. My first thought at the time was (and is still now upon reflection) that of seeing the tow-truck driver himself as the angel who arrived in time to tow the car out. There are many accounts—some you will read here in this book—of people who show up suddenly during a crisis, then seemingly disappear before they can be thanked for saving a life or rescuing someone from a dire situation. People often describe this feeling they have around the event as peculiar and phenomenal. They hold within themselves thereafter a quiet knowing that the person who heroically showed up and quickly disappeared from sight had to be an angel.

It is easy to see how I felt that the tow-truck driver himself was an angel in disguise. It is humorous and fun to play with that thought, thinking of an angel materializing from spirit form to a very human, earthy guy in his mid-forties with a well-used tow truck, complete with cinnamon whiskers on his unshaven face. Impossible as it may seem, the effect on me is still the same, and therefore "angelic"—my plight was drastically improved, as if by magic.

How likely is it that the guy suddenly appeared *for us* to be towed out of this situation before nightfall? The car spun, miraculously a tow truck appears, and then the tow guy towed us out and got paid fifty dollars. Now, that's where more interesting (and funny) questions arise. Okay, the fifty dollars . . . the very thought of an angel accepting cash from us is laughable, assuming where angels come from our currency is hardly anything but useless and most certainly vulgar. But I'll say now, angels might definitely take money or do other practical things we all do here on Earth for good reasons. For example, let's say the reckless driver of the car that spun out needed a smack in the wallet to wake up and realize he was endangering himself and others with his risky driving (and money talks, as they say; losing some money that day may have made an impression on him).

But let's look at this event that I felt was angelic from another angle. Could it also have been *an angelic event for the tow-truck driver*, who may have been just a regular man who needed an extra fifty dollars that day? From this perspective, we (the unsafe driver and myself, the passengers of the vehicle that spun into a ditch) could be considered the tow-truck driver's "angels." Seeing it from the tow-truck driver's possible viewpoint, he may have just prayed for some extra cash when a car in front of him miraculously spun out and needed his services immediately. After the event, that guy may have driven off thinking we were the answer to *his* prayers, wondering if we were angels in disguise.

Is it terribly naïve of all of us to go around thinking each other angelic beings? I'd say not really, because we can all play roles for one another in ways that truly do help make the world better, and the angels know this and do work through us.

I will never know for sure all the facts around what happened that day. But let's consider that angelic operatives may simply have been at work through all of us as regular hapless humans fumbling around hoping for things to run along smoothly with our lives. And my experience of the event was a "Godsend," meaning that I don't even have to prove angels are real in order to just be glad the situation was inexplicably good for me that day. My inward knowing tells me that prayers get answered and our guardian angels are trying to help us gain insight and consciousness and can either work directly through us, or can assume form and shape to help us.

What matters is how each of us *experiences the situations* we get into and the personal meaning we find in our circumstances. All we know and all we need to know, really, is that some things occur "just right" to keep a bad thing from becoming worse, and often we are saved from serious trouble or aided in a moment of dire need. The hows and whys of it are often inscrutable or even unfathomable.

This magic tow-truck moment and other accounts of angelic encounters lead me to think we should be interested in noticing the many ways in which we have inexplicably great kismet. Yet, it isn't just coincidence or luck. Angels protect and guide us; they often intervene by taking material form and shape or by influencing positive outcomes, sight unseen.

So the answer to the question "Is there really such a thing as angels?" is *yes*! Not just for those raised to believe in them or those who developed an affinity with the idea of angels, but even more so for those who have experienced life events so unusual that the only explanation that makes sense to them is to accept that their lives are at times touched by forces more mysterious than they know and more sacred than they thought possible. Many of us may frequently lament our ordinary, dusty, little, pathetic, wretched, lonely lives that we think can't be touched by angels. If we can be dramatic like that at times and feel deeply lost or ruined, then we need to be just as dramatic about the wispy, golden, silver, silent, unseen, magical presence of tender mercies upon us, too. For every little worry you have, put a wish on it for love, for kindness, for sweetness. It is part of the human condition to suffer, and yet there is that within us which *cannot be destroyed*: our soul's essence and the angelic light that has moved us in meaningful ways and turned our gaze toward heavenly auspices since ancient days. We aren't the first suckers or poor saps to suffer, or to be in need of angelic guidance or to be swooped up and cradled by patrons of pure love. All around the world, we have an inheritance rich in the lore of wondrous angelic workings, to commingle with our contemporary accounts of angelic benevolence.

Benevolence is the momentous force angels work with. It's an energy unseen by us, like rays of moving light, that they ride and shape as they swirl in and out of our physically structured existence. Wherever life is, angels will forever be, as they are the agents of change, enlightenment, and transference of love and healing within our created universe. Look to the stars and know there are angels there. Kick the sand and know there are angels there, too. Fly through time and space in your imagination and envision a scene of cavemen and cavewomen as they discovered fire . . . perhaps an angel helped guide them to this knowledge. See in your mind's eye the future, your future—and know there is an angel there who sees who your fully realized self will come to be, and this angel welcomes you forward into new phases of life.

Just as with our deepest, most private feelings, an angel is present. Go as far out and beyond as you can in your thoughts of Earth and the universe, and know that even out in the unperceivable darkness, angels soar.

ANGEL FACT: *Lamentation*, a fresco painting by Giotto at the Scrovegni Chapel in Padua, depicts winged angels appearing in the clouds, exhibiting expressions of pure grief.

2

angelic influences from the great expanse

You may have angels from far-flung galaxies, spaces, places and times, or other dimensions and worlds. And you may have an angel who is very much a close friend, someone who you feel immediately familiar with and open to, like anyone you might meet in your neighborhood or school or work. You may have an angel from somewhere across the globe, who appears in dreams or visions.

A GRANDMASTER GUARDIAN ANGEL

When I was pregnant with my first child, I didn't know if the baby was a boy or a girl. I had a dream that I was walking at night through a forest, and I came to a circular clearing and saw to my left a beautiful baby boy with dark hair lying in a little woodland cradle. I was so drawn to him. I approached him with such a surge of love and maternal protectiveness and suddenly thought, *Wait a minute, what is an innocent baby doing here all alone in the forest?!* I looked up and saw a robed wizard. He was Asian and smiling. He was turned toward me, facing the night sky, and he looked at me, then at the baby, and then up to the full moon. He then looked back at me. I telepathically knew he was telling me who the baby was (a little dark-haired infant boy) and he was telling me where the baby came from (the galaxy, stars, and moon—somewhere magical and far away). I knew when I woke up that this extraordinary guardian was the angel for this baby boy, asking me and urging me to take care of the baby. He was assigning me this wondrous opportunity to care for this infant. From that point on, I never forgot that my baby had this ancient, wise, and kind protector—a Grandmaster, a wizard! And when the baby was born, he was exactly as I had been shown: a baby boy with dark hair. He looked exactly as he had in the dream!

Stories like my own, of angels appearing in dreams to deliver messages, is not new. Angels were told of then and now. You can easily receive angel messages through your dreams and in other ways as well. (See more on dreams and angels in Chapter 9, page 79.) All over the world for centuries, people have developed a sense of receiving spiritual guidance or divine persuasion in the form of otherworldly messengers. No matter where humans have occupied Earth, there is a notion of atmospheric and unseen divine agents, spirits embodying humans or animals and presences within nature, all watching out for humankind. All we have to do is be open to receiving them and to formally journal or log our experiences so we get into the habit of noticing rather than ignoring the signs and messages.

A GLOBAL IDEA: POSITIVE AND NEGATIVE ANGELS

However, in most if not all cultures, as in our vast, mysterious universe, there is a dynamic of negative influences working against positive; angels of light and angels of shadow. So along with all the comforting advocates, we see a lot of troublemakers, too. In various creation myths and sacred scriptures, as well as in pop culture, we often see forces of light and dark battling, whether it be tiny people with furry toes in the Shire or federations and empires in distant galaxies. Humankind has had an understanding of the dual nature of the universe, the yin and the yang, for thousands and thousands of years. Since not all angels are helpful in the way we'd imagine them to be, the mischievous or even thoroughly evil ones are equally a part of a pantheon of angelic types and archetypes. Stories of angels, whether good or evil, can be discovered and explored on every continent.

The ancient and contemporary lore and religious belief systems as well as the modern personal accounts of angels is fascinating to learn about, and even more fascinating is your own personal experiences with angelic beings. Often, I've found that the script for angels that is common is not anywhere near the full spectrum of possibility—they're definitely not limited to chubby cherubs and winged ladies in robes.

In Western Abrahamic culture, we look to ancient Judaism for origins of the notion of angels in Torah, which greatly influenced the Christian and Islamic concept and practices of evoking angels as well as providing us with their characteristics and ways of intervening. The Judaic mystical spiritual structure, including angelic principles, is known as the Tree of Life (in Hebrew *Etz Chayim*,) and depicts the ten Sefirot, which we each embody, as Ein Sof, Creator of all life physical and the ethereal, reveals aspects of Himself to us.

From the teachings and classes of Kabbalah scholar and teacher Justin Beck:

> Kabbalah teaches that there is a structure to the universe and that angels are an integral part of this system. They guide us, send us messages, and intervene when necessary, working through us and around us. Angels facilitate the circulation of energy throughout the universe, having a direct impact on everything that happens in the world, no matter how big or small.

There are ten levels of angels in Kabbalistic teachings. The difference between levels is how well they comprehend the consciousness of their own existence. Most have nothing to do with our realm of existence—they operate in higher worlds. There are four major angels (see more about the archangels in Chapter 3, page 25).

GABRIEL: judgment/angel of strength

MICHAEL: messenger/angel of kindness

RAPHAEL: angel of healing

URIEL: angel of light

"According to the Zohar," says Beck, "one of the angels' designated tasks is to transport our words of prayer and Torah study before G-d's throne."

Beck teaches that there are both positive and negative angels at work all around us. He says:

> Which angels you attract depends upon *your actions*. According to the Zohar [Kabbalah text that is a mystical interpretation of the Pentateuch or Torah/ Hebrew Bible] when you hurt someone, break a trust, or act cruelly, you beckon destructive angels in your life. Conversely, when you share openly and commit acts of loving kindness, you attract positive angels and Light. Therefore, you are directly responsible for the angelic forces influencing your life.
>
> These positive and negative forces existed in the world long before we were here. Some of the best-known angels, according to ancient Jewish mysticism, have existed forever: the Angel of Death, Archangels, and Guardian Angels. Each category of angels serves different purposes. While angels may step in to save your

life, they can also help take you to the next step in your spiritual evolution. Sometimes a problem is solved "mysteriously" or a "coincidence" leads things to turn in your favor. Other times, an angel can come to you as an ordinary person. An angel disguised as an acquaintance or passerby can be someone who encourages you to take a different direction or asks you a question that leads to deeper introspection. They could even require assistance, giving you the opportunity to bring Light into the world and attract more positivity.

According to Kabbalah, a guardian angel escorted your soul into this world at birth and travels at your side until your death. Throughout your life's journey, your Guardian Angel is a friend, teacher, and spiritual partner steering you back on track when you stray. The more you open yourself to his or her influence, the more Light you can bring into the world, the more positive connections you will make, and the more doors that will open to you. They help us attain levels we couldn't achieve acting individually.

In his teachings, Beck helps us understand the way negative influences may indeed actually help us. He says:

Just as your Guardian Angel encourages your spiritual growth, your Negative Angel acts as your opponent, drawing you toward destructive behavior and pressuring you to indulge your ego. The actions you take in the face of resistance have a direct impact on your spiritual growth and transformation. Your Negative Angel brings your strengths and weaknesses into full view. Deep self-awareness allows you to maximize your merits and minimize your shortcomings. As a result, your Negative Angel gives you the opportunity to better your life and expand your consciousness.

The essence of the angels is within each of us (burgeoning to be realized). When we overcome the desire to receive for the self alone, we become similar to the essence of angels, the best version of ourselves possible.

Understanding how angels influence and affect our lives is imperative to spiritual growth. Angels are ever-present tools for transformation. Whether or not you are conscious of them, angels will continue to influence your life and the lives of those around you. In order to create joy and fulfillment and resist chaos, one can pray to G-d to empower the angels to complete their mission to the fullest without any hindrance or delay.

Getting a feeling for and a cozy sense of the archangels and lesser angels is a great idea, because you will begin a conscious, inner dialogue enveloping the attributes of the angels into your own essence. An awareness of how your personal counsel of angelic guides surrounds you and streams through you is essential to a buoyant and abundant life filled with incorporeal knowing and seeing. You won't regret it when you feel how much fun it is to be knowingly connected to benevolent spiritual presence.

Get to know these angels, because they belong to you!

HIERARCHY OF ANGELS: ANGELS OF THE TEN SEFIROT

CHAMUEL: This angel represents love through strength and knowing when to swiftly draw boundaries. Chamuel's love is decisive and can eliminate that which has a destructive or negative effect on the whole of a situation or person.

GABRIEL: Gabriel represents courage and the necessary destruction of that which is harmful to humans (sin) in the eyes of God. Some attributes of Gabriel are fierceness and decisive action. He is often depicted with a horn or trumpet.

HANIEL: Angel of joy, tenderness, and feminine expression of the divine, Haniel encourages empathic intelligence and the inner knowing that is easy to ignore but is often the in-dwelling Spirit urging us toward God.

METATRON: Metatron is considered the highest form of angel, having earned it during life as Enoch the scribe. He was transformed to the status of angel and sits at the Crown of the Tree of Life, influencing all aspects of human life.

MICHAEL: One of the most beloved archangels (also made a saint), Michael represents protection, swift and serious. In Kabbalah, he represents kindness and loving gestures that restore kindness among humans.

RAPHAEL: Raphael is a healer angel and removes evil or negative influences on mind, body, and soul.

RAZIEL: Raziel is called the Angel of Mysteries and is said to know the secrets of the universe. Raziel is also said to have written the first book and helps with personal revelation, as mysteries are revealed to us in divine timing according to our readiness.

SANDALPHON: This angel is the very powerful counterpart to Metatron and handles the earthy, material-based life forms, directing humans toward God from their place as physical beings via creative expression. Potential and harmony through creativity are some aspects of Sandalphon.

TZAPHKIEL: This angel brings healing of physical and mental energy through compassion and forgiveness. The name Tzaphkiel means "knowledge of God," and the pure energy of Tzaphkiel is that of unconditional love.

Other angels include those from the Book of Enoch: Uriel, Saraqael, Raguel, Remiel, and the seraphim and cherubim.

As you acquaint yourself with the angels and their attributes, you might experience this knowledge, gradually, more as a kind of reminder of what you already inwardly knew. These angels and the soul power they bring us dwell within humans at the core and root and are not foreign to us but rather one in being with us.

The ancient knowledge of these angels has been passed down to us over the centuries, allowing their influence to fortify humans spiritually, emotionally, and physically. Applying the knowledge personally will have a great impact on your life. You will see changes in your personality and shifts in your life dynamic. Your awareness of help from angels will give you a feeling of true companionship and love. Often, when we feel unhappy, stuck, or frustrated, we are actually feeling disconnected. When we are welcoming and notice the influence of angels, that disconnected feeling begins to fade. You will find that anxiety and pain begin to fade away, giving over to a lovely, soothing response in the face of a wide range of situations and people. Instead of being owned by someone's words or actions and reacting with vengeance, hurt, or anger, you will see that you respond differently, as though surrounded by a golden presence This is a wonderful sensation because it means you are no longer subjugated to the whims of others, the weather, or politics. You do not have to do, be, and fix all things.

At times, though, this angelic guidance may infuse you with the urge to act; it does not mean that loving angels and being in their presence makes us passive wimps who separate from fellow humans or world events. At times you will feel disturbed by life and have to rise up and speak out or take bold action. Angels do this themselves! They act swiftly on our behalf, and so must we at times be courageous in life to help others. Angels support us as we communicate our highest ideals and act with integrity based upon the virtues and ethics we consider good and fair for ourselves and others. Their actions heal and embolden the power of oneness, empathy, and valor.

Study the angels to incorporate their strengths of varying kinds into your own life and personal foundation, and you will most likely discover that you are more drawn to some than others. During a period of conflict, you may realize that Tzaphkiel's healing through compassion and forgiveness is exactly what you need. In times of injustice, you may see the angelic spirit of Gabriel come forth and encourage you to blow your own horn in defiance of wrongs done unto yourself or others. Trust your own gravitation to specific angels. You will feel a sense of peace even in times of making brave decisions.

ANGEL FACT: In Torah, when the Egyptian army pursued the Israelites and was defeated, drowning in the sea, the angels wept. The message here may be to never celebrate the death of people, who are God's creation—even your enemies.

3
nature angels

If you want to have knowledge of angels and cultivate an awareness of angels in your daily life, you're going to have to ask for it. Before reading this chapter, take a few deep breaths and ask for angels to show themselves to you. I always ask God to send me the angel that would be best for me. I ask for the ability to perceive and come to know these angels. Try it! In your own words, ask for angels to be present in ways that you can feel, see, hear, and sense. Journal anything unusual that happens. . . .

When I first began truly experiencing angels in a day-to-day way that was different from occasional random sightings and other angel events, it was because *I asked for it*. I had been ill with Lyme disease and had to spend many days in bed. I had to surrender everything during that time due to the illness. By "surrender everything," I mean I had to let go of any of my ego identification. I had to stop being "the artist" or "the author" and, in some ways, even my most important role of mother, because I was in bed and unable to fulfill those roles during the illness. I knew that I was being pulled close to the Source of Life because I could feel it. Through the illness, I was being given an opportunity to grow spiritually, which was a life-changing opportunity to transcend myself and my ego.

I remember the moment. I was lying in bed and could not even tolerate the feeling of the sheet on my skin, so sensitive was my nervous system at times with this terrible disease. Giving up on trying to control what I could not, I asked in prayer, out loud, to be shown angels. This began a wondrously fascinating and sacred adventure for me, and my life shifted.

If you'd truly like to have angels help you with your knowing through cooperation and you'd really like to have awareness of their presence, *ask for it*. Say a prayer in your own words and in your own way and ask to be shown. I asked for "whatever You think I'm ready for," and when I got my answer a few days later, I thought of the funny thing I learned years ago visiting Tuskegee, Alabama, and the science lab of George W. Carver. Carver had said that when he asked in prayer to understand the secrets of the universe, God's reply was that he wasn't big enough to know the secrets of the universe, but that he was big enough to know the secrets of the peanut!

So after I asked to be shown whatever God thought I was ready for, I expected to see major things such as Heaven, the beginning of Creation, and the Archangels, but instead I was first shown the most basic of all: nature angels.

NATURAL IS SUPERNATURAL

I woke up and opened my eyes softly, remaining still, and saw hovering over the bed, a few feet away from me, two colorful hologram-like apparitions. One was what I'd call a flower fairy. She was exactly as you'd imagine a fairy to be: Her skirt was made of long, delicate flower petals; she was dainty and lovely, like a ballerina. She embodied the feeling of sensual femininity. She telepathically communicated to me that she was radiantly resplendent (and she was!), full of supreme life energy, and a Godly beauty, and she expected me to know that. I gasped. To her left was the most erect little soldier of a man. And he was the epitome of "masculine." He, too, was a plantlike figure, only I can't say what type exactly. His expression was fierce. He stood like a general, legs apart, arms bent with his fists on his hips. He communicated to me that I had better know without a doubt that he was powerful and feisty and should not be toyed with at all.

As I stared at them and gradually began to question what I was seeing, they faded from view. I felt I was being shown the most basic of spiritual entities in our world, the elemental, foundational spirits that dwell in our natural world of growing, budding plant life.

All that day I thought of what I had seen. I was surprised! "My God," I said to myself, "the ancient tales of fairies and elves and things like that—they were right! They knew!" They must have seen these nature spirits for centuries, and what we assumed were just tales were actually truths: truths about our creation, our natural surroundings. We are pistils, stamens, and pollen; we are a growing, green, verdant, feminine and masculine world. And what I came to truly get for the first time was how adamantly desirable and lovely a flower is. A flower will not and cannot be anything but pure beauteous, budded, gloriously presented splendor. With magnificent confidence it allows life and utter wonderment to quest through it. A flower knows no other way.

We should know no other way as well! What the two nature spirits had shown me and communicated to me telepathically was a simple truth of our universe—that which is alive has the powerful duty to thrive in its natural compulsion; a living thing must simply *be* itself to the hilt. A flower does not apologize for its loveliness. In that gift of self that it offers, we are adorned beholding its exquisite angelic power. Through nature, we are fulfilled and given pure sexual life-force energy, without question or compromise.

Why is it that we humans forget our basic nature of creative life-force energy and make ourselves afraid to be bold with life? More often we are insecure and doubtful, and we cower and criticize ourselves or others, not allowing our true blooming nature to be expressed. Or, conversely, we bombastically overstate ourselves to prove our worth to the point of damaging what is tender and good. All we need to do is to be purely in our element—unafraid to allow the creative force of life to stream through us—and aware that, in opposition to commercial sales pitches or magazine headlines, we truly are beautiful as we are and are not lacking. Nature angels are among us to teach us by their doing, by their example of being exactly as they are through the living substance they inhabit. And we, through our appreciation of them, will be able to recognize the miracle of life better, to feel it and celebrate it in ourselves as well as in every living thing.

My angelic personal tutorial on the basics of nature angels has continued. I keep seeing, hearing, and sensing the many ways angels come through for our benefit. Not long after being shown the delicate, feminine, and powerful flower angel and the assertive, self-reliant masculine angel, I was shown angels who commingle with the elements as they urge us toward bounty. They live in Technicolor abundance right beside us, but in another dimension. They are very present, but invisible and undiscernable to us. They are in our midst trying to help us cultivate all growing things, especially food—vegetables and fruits, grains, seeds, legumes. They are like a multi-racial commune of spiritual nurturers who beam with goodness as they plant and harvest that which is edible to us, compelling us to want to garden, to grow our own food, and to delight in the stunning beauty of plant life. We can't hear, sense, or feel them unless we tune inward and receive the signals they send. When we feel the compulsion to cultivate growing life, especially vegetables and fruit, this is their angelic influence working through us. We have become so separate from this since we get our sustenance at the grocer's rather than being an integral partner in growing, from seed to ripeness. Nature angels are urging us back to these basics to save us and teach us to survive anew, without depending on suppliers to grow and sell the food we eat. The feeling was that we have become so dependent on outside structures to provide sustenance that we would not survive long if, say, the power grid went out for a week or some other calamity occurred. These angels urged us to desire and learn to grow food for ourselves.

HOW TO CONNECT WITH NATURE ANGELS

Go outside frequently, and breathe deeply. To be alive is to breathe. And whether in a rural, suburban, or urban environment, you should connect to any kind of nature that may be around you. Bring plants into your house so you can be blessed by their beauty. Wherever you are, delight in the clouds, the feeling of the air, the limbs of the trees, and every bud or leaf you encounter. Being indifferent to these angels in nature is to be unalive, and you want to talk to, sing to, and honor the natural life you see around you. If you think you'll be hauled away on insanity charges for serenading a flower, whisper your song or sing it in your heart. Otherwise, it's worth the risk.

Meander and savor the feeling of lightness and sweetness that growing things give us. Take in the deep green hues, and you may quietly approach trees, feeling blades of grass—each one, as the Talmud states, with its own angel—urging it to grow, grow! Breathe easy; walk with a sense of calm excitement. You are among the majestic. Notice birds and animals, rocks and moss. They each have angelic presences and are gifts to us. If you see an animal, look up the symbolism to find the meaning. An animal may have crossed your path, delivering an angelic message to support you in some way, or to guide you.

Go outside knowing that there is a message—perhaps many—there for you. Feel yourself being filled with appreciation, and do not forget to tell each leaf or branch, stone or bud how ravishingly splendid it is in its beingness.

ANGEL FACT: Seraphim angels have wings that cover their faces because God is so holy that they cannot look upon Him.

4

you're very attractive: negative and positive angels

If we have personal angels, can we have the kind we'd like to have? I would like to have angels to help me with my creative work. At other times, I'd like an angel to send me surprises in the way of romance. Or career. Or to find people I feel great around. What about you? What kind of angels would you like to have enhance your life, light up your path, and give you knowledge and guidance? We have to work with both positive and negative forces of spiritual nature. So it is important to understand that we can attract all kinds of angel momentum. Are we gaining the kind of propulsion that we feel is best for us? (We all know that dreadful feeling of everything rolling with great momentum in just the way we hoped it would not.) What do we do to generate the kind of spiritual forces that feel in sync with our hopes?

Being consciously aware of how we set ourselves up dynamically helps us greatly. And our angel energies are part of every situation in which we find ourselves. Let's look at angels, both positive and negative, since we learn from both during the course of our lives.

ENCHANTED: NEGATIVE ANGELS

As we learned in the previous chapter about the Tree of Life, there are both positive and negative angels and spiritual forces. What exactly is a "negative" angel? And why would we even have them? Subversive spirits are said to be everywhere. Our world is one of duality, dark and light, good and evil, nighttime and daytime. For every speck of life there is an indwelling angel of light and an indwelling angel of shadow. A positive angel and a negative one. A sublime one and an erroneous one. A healing one and a sickening one. We learn from all of them. We choose among them our entire life. And we even create them, good and bad, beauty and beast. Somehow, through our journey of days, angels of pain and struggles, the cruel and the grotesque ones, teach us through experience. The corrections we make as we emerge from struggle and pain soothe our souls through choosing light over darkness. Emerging from pain into relief, from illness into health, and from hate into love is why we are alive.

EGO IS ALSO A GIFT

Our egos are part of who we are and how we learn. The ego sets us up for a lot of life lessons. We have to overcome it, but it is there for us.

Is it fair to say that human beings are enraptured with the ego-driven allure of sex, wealth, power, and a sense of supreme omnipotence in the way of intellect, beauty, or magnetic prowess? One or more of these compelling delights is what usually does us in. We are not hard to seduce, and we have fun seducing. Our egos demand that we prove our superiority, but the ego will also berate us constantly. As we grapple and wrestle with our ego's demands, we suffer one holy headlock after another until we triumph. To triumph means to override the ego's assessment of our specialness and of the ego's shaming us into believing we never have enough, win enough, or do enough. We are trapped on a carousel of having to prove ourselves out of fear of failure, until we receive a grace that angels so mercifully surround us with and pour into us by their presence and interventions in our lives.

Selfie

When we've attracted a negative angel, we find how easily opportunities to feed the beastly ego draw near. Every day is then made up of convincing someone, if not the world, of how bewitching we are ("Look how sexy I am"). And proving our beguiling uniqueness is our ego's constant strategy. So we compete with others, hell-bent on "winning." To the ego, all of Earth life is a constant "I win" or "I lose" game. This is exhausting. It can't be all there is to life! Even just passing someone on the sidewalk. You'll notice some people pretend others in their midst don't exist, as if to refuse to acknowledge they're there, while others may offer a kind smile or a nod or even a hello. The ego seeks to have a sense of superiority even in such small passing encounters as that—and will consider itself "winner" when ignoring others.

Another version of this is when someone may need to feel they "win" by charming everyone—or by charming a target person, then conquering and ultimately destroying the target person's sense of themselves, their self-esteem, or their ability to function. These things often take years and years to play out. The ego is that powerful over our lives. Once we agree to let this smoky aspect of our humanness ravage all parts of us, we don't win anything at all. We lose the chance to know what love is.

Angels of positive energy will not give up on us, and they understand that we have stages of maturation and that the ego, too, is a gift of God, and that through our pride or ambitions we learn many, many soul lessons. We learn through loss and pain, or not. Either way, the angels of peace and love will not let us down, even while we frolic only with the angels of destruction.

How Do You Get Sucked In to Negative?

When at play with consumptive, detrimental angels, more deception keeps coming your way. It is as if a magnet is on your head sending signals near and far, to town and country, that *you* are game for some deceptive or unseemly activity. These little negative angels get generated and attached to your own similar and matching thought forms. These are like small angels you've created. Along with the angels you've summoned, they keep pulling you in and drawing you toward more of the same. You may be so "into it" that you don't even realize this is happening until the pressure builds up, or the scheme implodes, or misery weighs you or others down, causing you to "see the light" and change course—in other words, until the angels, however negative, fulfill their purpose.

SOME WAYS WE ATTRACT SHADOW ANGELS

- Forcing your will
- Exclusion of others
- Deception
- Lying
- Stealing
- Cheating
- Holding on to anger
- Holding on to guilt
- Agreeing to be weak
- Agreeing to remain wounded
- Manipulation of others for selfish reasons
- Invoking outright negative spirits
- Cruel humor
- Dominating others
- Disliking or using young children
- Sexual exploitation (using others for or through sex)

ADORNED: POSITIVE ANGELS

Angels of refined spiritual beauty have a dignity that we recognize at times within ourselves, and we see it in others who have come through difficulty or adversity and emerged whole. This dignity is held in the posture, in the forbearance of individuals who were not validated by the outer world (a relationship or community of some kind) but who came through their own human imperfection to emerge as noble in humility, with courage and elegance of essence.

Positive angels leave signs everywhere in the way of unconditional love and playfulness. They call us to our higher selves, while we rest or carry on with daily duties, during recreation or work, making our tasks lighter, even a joy. They may come in dreams, or through lines in a movie you just happened to turn on at the exact moment to hear words that have an impact on you. They come through in small ways and large.

Angels Know What You Need

A teenage boy told me about having a plowing job with a friend and how, during a dangerous blizzard very early in the morning, angelic assistance came easily. It was total white-out conditions and as the two teens drove to start their plowing jobs, which were hazardous and important, they realized they needed electrical tape but didn't have any. No stores would be open, the state was basically shut down and there was no way they could just find the tape they needed.

"Just then," the teenager said, "we saw two kids in pajamas and winter coats, standing in their driveway." The driver of the plow truck said, "Hey wait, I know those kids! Let's ask them if they have electrical tape." They stopped and said hello and asked the kids if they could borrow some electrical tape. Within moments, they had been given the tape and were on their way through the blizzard to do their jobs. The two marveled at how unlikely it was that kids in their pajamas would be outside in the blizzard and how they seemed to be out there "just for us," as they put it. Both boys felt touched by this experience and felt that angels had helped them. This was a very positive angelic encounter, when what was needed was provided effortlessly.

How Can You Attract Positive Angels?

If you're creating positive thought forms and if or when the greater part of your ego has died like the Wicked Witch of the West, melting at your feet, angelic companions of love and forgiveness divinely provide you with all the good you deserve. They'll soothe you in the suffering you have known.

But guess what: Even after overcoming the drive to win at all costs against another, you will still be given opportunities to slip into and cavort with the shadow angels. But because your resident angels are corrective, healing, and positive forces, you will realize and see the "evil inclination" angels for what they are, and you will pause, reflect, and most likely choose to steer clear of the dark.

Yet, let's say even as you have bathed in the waters of clarity and peace, an invitation and opportunity to venture into a temptation via a slightly mischievous scheme (one that seems harmless) is accepted by you. Your constructive angel presences that you have held close by with your good will and intentions will try to limit your ability to follow through on the murky plan that you are considering. These positive angels will make the timing wrong (think of the would-be bank robber), they'll frustrate the way it all plays out, so you get more chances to free yourself of the pernicious web entangling you.

Same goes for us if we continually swim in the bog of gritty dealings. The thrills will wear off, the chances to unveil will be offered. Angels of mercy and kindness will try to loosen the greasy grip of adverse actions from your life.

SOMETIMES A "BAD THING" IS A "GOOD THING" WITH YOUR ANGELS

Since we know an angel has to use what seems very unfavorable if not downright "bad" for the purpose of good sometimes, it is very gainful to stop and reflect when something we'd call dreadful, lousy, or annoying happens. Below is an example of the way in which this can unfold in our day-to-day encounters.

Two Wrongs Make a Right

I had a flat tire. My teenage son kindly changed the tire before he left for school, replacing it with the spare. The spare turned out to be flat. This was very upsetting. I had a choice to make—to get angry and fume all the way to the dealership (which was the closest place to drive to have the tire fixed, as it would cost me way more than just taking the car to a tire shop) or to calm down and stay positive. I had a few moments there to consider that I could still remain cheerful in spite of the downer of the day, two flat tires. Picture me, on one hand, with negative angels poised, ready, and perhaps even eager for me to create more little fiery beastly angels through my thoughts and emotions of anger, despair, frustration, and discomfort. And picture me, on the other hand, with harmoniously serene and tranquil angels, enveloping me with the graceful acceptance of my circumstances, or at least with a sense of humor around the discomfort of expensive bad news.

On this day, for some reason, I decided to align with the angels of grace and thought of making the best of this situation. I slowly drove, basically on the rim of the flat spare, a few blocks away to the car dealership.

Inside the receiving area, an attendant asked me what my problem was that day. I said, "I have a flat tire."

He said, "Okay," and started typing on the computer.

Then I said, "And the spare is flat," he looked up at me, and we both started laughing. Then he said, through a beautiful grin, "What's your name so I can find you in our system?"

And I said, still smiling, "Oh. It's probably under my ex-husband's name." More laughter burst from the both of us. My life seemed very unlucky (and funny). He then said he'd get the mechanics to fix both. I was led to the waiting room that smelled like rubber and grease and there was a TV on.

I was waiting, getting agitated (more negative angels?) because an insurance company's commercial kept airing over and over. I felt I was in purgatory, but I closed my eyes and decided to be patient. Eventually, the attendant came and got me, and I said, "I'm so glad you're here. If I have to listen to this commercial one more time, I'll die." This attendant and I seemed like best friends for life the way we were laughing at my circumstances.

He then said, "Well, your tires are both fixed. *And* we found that *your car did not have any oil*! It is a good thing you brought it in, because your engine would have locked up at any moment if you hadn't done so."

I was astonished, and said, "Oh gosh, I must have a really good guardian angel," and he agreed. Then he gave me the bill, which I took over to the window to make my payment. There the woman took my bill and said, "No charge today!" I was aghast. Why were they not charging me for fixing two tires and putting oil in my car? I walked out on a cloud; I was so happy that I can't even express it fully. I knew that if I had not had a flat spare as well as the other flat tire, I'd have driven on the spare tire possibly for days, I'd have taken my time getting to a tire place (where they would not have checked my oil) and my car engine would have been destroyed for lack of oil. Two flat tires suddenly seemed like a very good thing!

What was a very bit of bad luck was actually my guardian angel in disguise, giving me the best gift ever. And since I trusted it and didn't play into a more typical response (cursing, being snippy with everyone, going into the dealership with a gloomy or irritated attitude, etc.), I had one of the best days ever. I smile inside and outside every time I think of it.

IF YOU WANT THEM TO COME HERE, YOU'VE GOT TO GO THERE

We attract angels whether we know it or not. When we are not conscious of this, we still attract them by our daily diet of positive versus negative substance. In other words, what we take in, eat up, or gravitate to gives us a good idea of the kind of energies we are absorbing, and along with that come the angels. The things we give our attention to are enormous influencers to us.

To attract positive angels, to increase your awareness of these sacred, airy beings, and to develop a daily practice of welcoming them in your life, you've got to be like the child you once were: innocent, open. You've got to feel imaginative, playful, and easygoing. You've got to let go of being "on task" and give yourself time to become a cloud, soft and floaty. Pay attention differently than the way you were conditioned in school. Be alert spiritually, with empathy stirring in your heart.

Take time daily to lie down and close your eyes. Feel yourself become a pink, puffy, misty fluff of cotton candy. Breathe deeply.

Release all your busy thoughts. Just *be*. If you're really relaxed, you should feel heavy at first, calm and peaceful, and then gradually you'll feel yourself slide away, as if on an astral conveyor belt or slip-and-slide ride. You are about to spiritually travel.

Close your eyes. What do you see? Is it dark and splotchy? When you relax and practice happily getting angel-ready, you will begin to see things in the darkness of your closed eyes. This will require you to be in a position of rest or ease. It will also require a bit of fearlessness. "Facing the darkness," of your eyes closed, you will allow your third eye to do some seeing for you. If you become so relaxed that you fall asleep, that is okay—there you will dream, which is a multidimensional blend of psychological, physiological, and spiritual forces at work.

Some ways we attract angels of light:

- Empathy
- Forgiving others
- Creative playfulness
- Kind curiosity about others
- Gentleness
- Courage
- Being in appreciation
- Doing good deeds for others
- Believing in your innate gifts
- Encouraging the strengths in others

ANGEL FACT: Angels throughout history have been said to sometimes have a gold, silver, or bronze appearance and wear clothes such as robes and sandals.

5
the angel aspects
in you

You have natural angelic energy flowing through you. It is not complex, really. To begin to reach the aspects within that empower your mind, body, and soul, say hello to your in-dwelling angelic guides.

CREATIVITY ANGEL: Your true nature is to create, create, create. You do it constantly, whether you create a meal, a report at work or school, or boredom by wandering around with nothing to do. It is all choices, and every gesture you make sets off a series of waves of creative force. This angel helps you create what you need to so that you may learn what you came alive as a human to learn. Get ready to get freely playful and expressive, even if what you have to create at the moment is your tax return. Do it with zeal and an affection for even the annoying things life has in it. Hold your hand at your crown and third eye (top of the head and middle of the forehead).

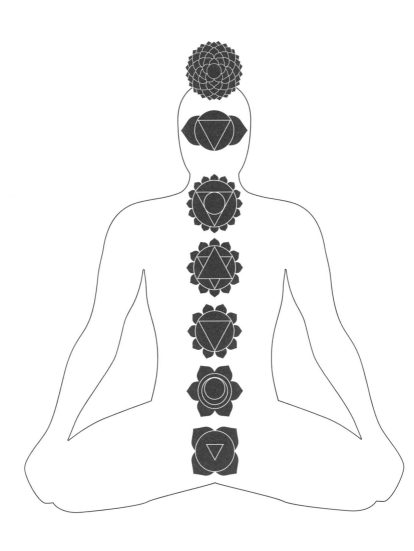

A LITTLE BIT OF ANGELS

Ask this angel of creativity to make you fearless of self-criticism and immune to the critical opinions of others, and ask yourself what you would love to create. And then go do it. It might be a collage. It might be to take a nap first (yes, a nap can be creative—when you may get your best ideas!). It might be to clear up an area of your space to make it more charming. But get creative, and get loose and happy with this angel!

EMPATHY ANGEL: Place your hand on your heart. Feel the energy that is held in that area of your body. The emotional energy stored there is usually very potent and may even be felt in your throat, as if a surge of feeling is pushed up from the heart. There is an angel in this area of your body, caring for you and helping you care for the feelings of others.

FORGIVENESS ANGEL: Place one hand on your heart and the other on your stomach. Forgiveness and an angel of mercy reside here, in the heart and solar chakra, or stomach area, where all your major organs harmonize to keep you healthy. Breathe deeply a few times, feeling the tension leave your solar plexus. You may have someone to forgive, or may even need to forgive yourself. Know that holy and specific spiritual reimbursement is yours when you allow yourself to forgive. The universe will give you back what you have lost tenfold. Forgive anyone who harmed you, or who betrayed you or someone you love. Feel yourself release (even if for a moment) the anger or pain you have associated with that person or situation. Tell yourself that you will receive divine compensation for the pain and loss, and will be able to receive that and so much goodness, once you release from your heart and solar plexus the feelings of emotional threat and sorrow. Practice connection with your very own forgiveness angel until you feel lighter and lighter. You may have to do this several times a day, but it will be worth it.

CREATIVE VISUALIZATION MEDITATION

Try this exercise to work with the angels that reside within. This meditation will clear and cleanse heavy emotions stored in your chakras.

Start by lying down so you are comfortable with your legs uncrossed and arms loosely resting at your sides. With your eyes closed, breathe deeply. Feel yourself become open. Imagine that you are a small pearl of water on the edge of a leaf, gently hovering over a brook. Feel yourself reflecting light and color.

Inhale and feel yourself drop from the very tip of the leaf and into the brook below. Now you are no longer a small droplet but are one with the flowing brook. Feel how you easily meander over rocks and twigs and through gentle turns. You are flowing and cannot be held back; there are no obstacles that will inhibit your current motion. Remember: You are not like the water, you *are* the water.

Flow happily until you merge into a far greater waterway: a mighty river. Feel the rush of exhilaration as it washes through you. You are one with a great river, rushing with joy, unstoppable. Allow yourself to once again flow over rocks and under branches. Feel the bubbles tingling like champagne at your crown, your temples, and in your throat, heart, and solar chakra. Feel the thrill of the white rapids in your sacral and primal chakras, straight down to your toes.

As you come bursting into the ocean, let the bubbles lather, pop, and foam into sunlit swirls. You may feel the temperature change from warm to cool. Picture yourself as the sea's glass-green water that mists into prisms. You are the prismatic colors; you are the sunlit splashes and the light and airy sea foam.

You might imagine rising into the sky as mist and entering a new realm that's your very own. Or you may see all the creatures living in your consciousness, all with surprises to reveal. Breathe easily and deeply knowing that, through this meditation, you have begun a journey into angelic creative realms, where wonderful imaginings fortify your soul and allow you to create what you love most here on Earth.

ANGEL FACT: The Native American Thunderbird is angel-like, helps humans, and delivers messages from Great Spirit. The mighty Thunderbird carries the power of lightning, which strikes through his eyes.

6
creating and visiting angelic realms

Before you read on, let's generate and create a positive angelic experience and attract some good stuff. First, think of something you love. It can be your favorite place, even a place you imagine. It can be a dream you have of becoming, it can be something ideal and wonderful to you. Think of it by holding it in your mind and heart, not feeling the lack of it. Now try imagining with me for a moment your absolute dream castle, which holds within it everything you love. See it exactly as you'd wish your dream castle to be, not as though it is a thing withheld from you, not like this, "Oh I wish I had a castle, but I don't and I'll never get one and I want one so badly but it isn't realistic and I live somewhere crummy now so it is impossible to ever have a castle and . . ." but rather "I just love castles. I love the turrets and the pink clouds like cotton candy that float above it and the moat and the rich dark wood inside and the lions carved on the door and the noble prince within who loves with all his heart the valiant queen who lives there, standing by a blazing fire in the hearth. . . ." (Think of it exactly as you'd like it, though my example is just some of what I'd have in mine!) Think of your dream castle and genuinely feel it as if you already have it, feel it like you're there: You smell it, you feel it under your feet, you see the surroundings in your mind's eye. You are in your dream castle.

CREATIVE VISUALIZATION IS YOUR MOST POWERFUL TOOL

Now, consider what you just did. You conjured in your mind a thing you treasure. If you love it, energetically you DO have it. All things get created "over there" where angels roam, before "over here" in 3-D. Even that chair you're probably sitting in that we mentioned earlier. Or the bed you're lying down on. All of it existed as an idea before it was created in material form. So enjoy your conjured place abundantly in your thoughts. Feel how good it is to feel you already have that which you love; it has immense potential.

With your great vibes, you just created a thought form of that very castle. You created the feeling of appreciation for something you love, and that feeling generated a spiritual as of yet nonphysical energetic presence, an angel. You just created a kind of "castle angel." This is how you both summon angels and make space for them in your days—by creating their presence through spiritual seeing, and integrating them into your identity where your will and intentions can work in harmony with angels. So, now, after this exercise, there is a "castle angel" that your spiritual intention and limitless imagination just conjured, and it is that easy.

What? I hear you, you're asking, "What in the world? What am I going to do with a castle angel?" The question is *what is the castle angel going to do with you?!* The castle angel is a soul thought-form you just gave from within, outwardly. It is filled with your love and appreciation for your ideals. Your ideal castle has a little thought form entity now, which you sent out into the world. And chances are that which you love, in "divine timing" or in "angel time," will come to you in some form. Maybe not all at once, and maybe not exactly as you saw it, but some of what you love and felt the deepest appreciation for is yours because you just made it yours as you held the feeling of it in your heart. And it was created in the ether, and will be created in various ways in your physical surroundings. Yes, it will.

CONNECT TO ANYONE THROUGH ANGELIC REALMS! CARY GRANT'S MOVIE THEATER IN MY DREAM CASTLE

I have a realm, with a castle and a Tree of Life in it where everything I love and want for myself and others exists. I started working on it once a few years ago when I was feeling unwell. I was in bed and a Cary Grant movie was on TV. I decided to have a Cary Grant movie theater in my realm. I mentally got to work on what this theater should look like. I gave it red drapes and a dramatic entrance. I set it up nice and plush and fun, with free candy and popcorn. But for the life of me, every time I entered this Cary Grant theater, it refused to be a movie theater for me. The red drapes fell away and a trapeze artist would come swinging through. There was no dark anticipation of a film about to start. Instead it was all lit up like a circus or something, and people were doing gymnastics and rehearsing jokes and things. I was very frustrated!

I decided I'd order some biographies of Cary Grant, since I had never read one before. Once the books arrived I had quite a shock. I read that Cary Grant left home at a young age to join a sort of vaudeville troupe or circus kind of traveling show. There was a quote that he actually said, upon reflection, that he didn't love making movies as much as he loved that first experience of show business, for all it taught him (!). He described how he learned comedy and gymnastic stunts, and performing this way really gave him happiness. I was so stunned. I realized that even in our most quiet, private thoughts, like closing our eyes and imagining a little realm, even there, angels can be present in the way of psychic or spiritual phenomena. How could I have had a theater dedicated to Cary Grant and actually have Cary Grant (seemingly so!) not allow it to be a theater in my mind, but a traveling circus—something *he* liked better—in *my* realm?

I was so surprised, but edified, too, because I realized we are truly one in that perhaps there is an anamorphic field where all of our thoughts and experiences exist, as if in a cloud, and we are able to access it and connect with others, those still alive but also total strangers who are no longer even alive on Earth—and all this in our mind's eyes or the imaginations of the heart. These are the languages of angels, the act of creation through spiritual means, and that substance of spirit is what animates our worlds—both the physical and the ethereal. What I learned here is not to suppose your imagination is isolated or flimsy. It is not. It is supremely powerful, more so than we could ever know. You might try experimenting with this. Is there someone famous you'd love to have met who once lived or even someone now you wish you could meet? Try doing so on angel turf—in the astral realm where anything is possible. And then watch for signs showing that connecting in an angelic way with anyone is possible!

ANGEL FACT: Celestial beings of light in Hinduism are known as *Devas* and are half-human, half-god. Some are associated with sound, and this is where the word *mantra* comes from, as in a prayer or meditation song.

7

your own personal angel: guardians among us

Different phases of life call for different types of protection and guidance. Understand that you are always covered by at least one angel, a messenger and guide, who works on your behalf. Remember, too, that your inclinations and intentions will influence what type of angels you will attract, but one in particular is assigned to you at birth and will be with you as you die, and that is your very own personal guardian angel.

The best way to understand, see, and feel your own guardian angel is to tune in and see what comes to you. Here are some ways to playfully, but with feeling, grasp who your guardian angel is:

- Ask a friend to meditate and see your angel. (This is fun and amazing.)

- Ask to be shown through a direct sign: nature, electronics, media, or other.

- Write a letter to your guardian angel. (Start a personal dialogue.)

- Speak openly to your guardian angel, out loud.

- Sing to your guardian angel.

- Dedicate your walk or exercise to receiving wisdom from your guardian angel. (This creates physical momentum toward your request.)

- Read about angels and see which one(s) you are most drawn to; the one you feel closest to is most likely one of your angels.

- Plant a garden or create something for your guardian angel.

- Ask to receive daily signs as to who your guardian angel is.

- Keep a dream journal so you can recall messages you may receive.

Growing up, I had a sense of a presence with me but it wasn't until I was older that I began to see a variety of spiritual beings who seemed to be protecting me and giving me the healing energy I needed.

THE EASYGOING ANGEL

When you're stressed, a de-stressor angel will start working through you. Don't doubt it for a moment; instead, be open to receiving signs and messages, and be open to that spiritual presence that will unwind you in sweet ways.

At one point after my sons were born, I was finding it hard to be both a mother and career person, and I had to feel my ego die a bit as I let go of some of my ambition as an artist and author in favor of truly focusing on the needs of my very young sons, who were two and four years old. It was a lesson in love. On weekends, though, I'd go into the studio and do my work, which always centers me and helps me feel balanced.

At one point, in a very vivid dream during this time, I was in my studio painting and a man was at the window, just chatting with me, and I felt we knew each other very well! He was African American, he was full of humor and joy, with a round, smiling face, and he was a little bit chubby. He was the most fun, easygoing person. He would just talk with me while I made art. The energy he gave me was not that of aggressive, ambitious goal-oriented severity (like my ego at the time), but rather a relaxed and pleasant, loving sense of goodness. I soaked it up. I kept looking over my shoulder at him as he leaned in from the outside, his elbows resting on the window casement. We talked and laughed. At one point I realized it was not possible for him to stand at my window like that. I said, "Hey, wait a minute— you're leaning in my window but this studio is on the second floor!" He smiled and shrugged and his eyes twinkled as he said, "Oh, I can be any height I need to be."

Angels often are very tall and can appear as giants, but can also be extremely small pinpoints of light. They are whatever they need to be for accomplishing their mission for and with us.

I Got Told!

I had only one other encounter with this loving angel who I believe came into my life at the right time to soothe me and teach me humility and acceptance of love on a new level, beyond the designs of the ego.

In this second encounter, he was angry with me, though. I had been meditating and instead of saying, in prayer, "God, send me whatever is best for me," as my mom and dad always taught me, I was willful and began asserting very forcibly that, like others had, I wanted to see an apparition of the Virgin Mary. I was raised Roman Catholic and after reading about Jesus as a Jew, and first-century Judaism, I was very much in love with the Jewish roots of Christianity. I felt very connected to Judaism in my heart (as I had been since my early twenties) and was looking for *proof* of the existence of Mary in my spiritual curiosity (looking for God to tell me facts about religion!).

As I sat alone during a thunderstorm one day, I was praying for God to show me Mary (over and over I repeated this command, not a request, a command), the sun came out and the storm passed. But then suddenly a loud explosion could be heard, a booming echo of thunder and flash of light, signaling that the lightning was directly overhead. It blew out the pool motor at our house, in fact. The lightning had struck very close by, even though the sun was out and the storm clouds had passed. I know lightning can do that, can strike even when we think the storm clouds have gone, but I inwardly wondered if somehow the conjuring of my wish like a little witch had in part caused this to happen. I dismissed it because of course we do not control the weather with our demands, but I still felt funny about it and as though I had somehow attracted a strong energetic response from nature or God.

That night, in my dream, I was somewhere with a lot of night-time colors, and this sweet angel buddy, the de-stressor angel who I came to appreciate so much, spoke to me in a very different way than he had previously. It made a mighty impression on me. With very stern words, he admonished me, "Don't push the river!" he shouted at me. "Don't mess with the time!" I woke up feeling very "told" and very put in my place. But I understood clearly what his message was. *We should not ask for what we are not ready for, since we will get it in some form.* Prayers get answered, and you know the saying "be careful of what you wish for." When we ask, we do receive that which we request, and if we are not ready for what we demand, we will muck up everything the angels are preparing for our soul purpose fulfillment. Better to ask for what we are ready for, as I did when I asked to start learning about the world of spirits, angels, and guides (and was shown the most basic angels—nature spirits).

Clearly, I was not ready—or it was not meant to be—to see an apparition of Mary! How very presumptuous of me to assume I could just ask in a pushy way like that.

Angels Follow Up

Sometime not long after this important angelic experience, I did have a powerful meditation that turned out to be related to my immature request. To my surprise, my request was answered, but not at all in the way I expected.

I found myself in meditation and saw a Native American powwow. Open in my mind's eye. I was looking out at the center of the powwow when the most beautiful woman glided in—glided, not walked. I was stunned and surprised. And it was the Virgin Mary! Tears immediately streamed down my cheeks, so gracious was she. And she was in Native American buckskin of a pale shade with beautiful ornate tribal designs on it. I received a gift that day, and that gift was feeling the deep love of the spirit of the feminine divine, omnipotent love that transcends race and encompasses all traditions and religions. I knew inwardly after that "visitation" that, at least for me, a feminine divine presence was able to give immense love in many shapes and forms. This is not meant to in any way take away from the Virgin Mary of Christianity, and I can only assume this love that struck my heart that day in a meditation powwow ceremony was given to me this way to show me that God's love finds us wherever we are, whoever we are in our seeking.

THE PERSONAL ASSISTANT AND EXPERT MANAGER ANGEL

At another phase of my life, when everything became difficult and a big family change was needed, a sudden move opened up for us. A new friend had a cottage available for us to rent while our home was refurbished and put on the market. It was a tough transition, but necessary. Once we got to the cottage, I dreamed of another guardian angel. This one was very metrosexual: He was unemotional, wore neutral colors of gray shades, and was not friendly and chatty at all like the easygoing angel had been. He was Caucasian and tall, had very neat, short dark hair, and was slender and "all business." And his business was getting me where I needed to be and whatever it was I needed, to the minute, to the second. He arranged everything, promptly and with absolute precision. Precision was his name, if he had one. He was silent, communicating more telepathically. As the dream story was told, I received the knowledge that many of the things that happened for me were indeed spiritually prearranged and set up for optimal effect by this emotionless, yet caring and dutiful, angel. I have not seen this angel since, but am certain if I need him again, he will show up exactly on time to help me.

ANGEL FACT: Angels in Renaissance art were depicted to look a lot like Cupid, the Greek god of love and eroticism. To capture the innocence of children (who are protected by the class of angels known as cherubim), artists in the 1500s started painting both angels and cupids to resemble adorable chubby-cheeked babies, known as cherubs.

8

it ain't easy: give your angel a break!

We can make it easy on our angels, or we can make it hard for them as they try to help us navigate our lives (as we saw in my de-stressor angel experience!). They have a sense of humor about us but they do also feel our pain most keenly. They passionately want us to be well. We all know that, at times, we may not do what we sense inwardly we should do but, instead, let ourselves slip into negative patterns or destructive ones. We have the inclination to satisfy our egos and ignore the angelic promptings to choose love and consideration for others. Why do we do that? I guess it is only human, and angels know that. We have lighter, happier days when we listen to the inner voice, when we hear and feel the gentle persuasion of the angels, and trust that even if it hurts to give up something the ego really badly wants, it will be way more rewarding in the long run. Receiving the angelic message and embodying it, we usually feel fortified in an unspoken way, and even in our suffering, we carry a kind of grace that we otherwise would never be in touch with or have as our own.

Either way, the angels will "be there" for us as they try to keep us in alignment with our soul, and no matter where we are in our soul journeys, love is still the ultimate answer, and even if we attract negative angels and create little spin-off negative angels, there is still an angelic order that guides us to that ultimate goal of love.

Our guardian angels in particular have to watch us flounder; they see us as we keep choosing "the pit" or the painful route, even when we kind of do know better. They watch us as we often choose as if we did not yet know *not to* choose poorly. Which must mean we still didn't know better, because once we have truly evolved, we simply do not choose ways that bring about pain or harm to others. It takes a lot of practice and a lot of mistakes before we learn.

Let's say some of us, if not most of us, somehow know, for example, that stealing money from a bank isn't a great idea, and we would never, ever try it. Others have not been convinced of that yet, and do rob banks. How is it that some people understand not to rob banks but others do not know the pain or misery or violence it may bring? Or even worse, they crave and desire the violence or excitement it brings them. Sometimes perhaps desperation or extreme deprivation may cause a person to develop the urge to steal and the skills to do so. Whatever the cause, we can surmise that the angels looking over the person entering a bank with a mask on and a gun, with the intention to steal money, have to either be shadowy angels, superb at helping their assigned human at robbing banks, or they have to be angels of light, of peace-energy, fretting, because their wayward human charge is making a big, big mistake. For the peaceful angel assigned to one who wills to do harmful acts, this has to be a tough angel assignment. But that angel will keep trying.

GUARDIAN ANGELS PREVENT A CRIME?

Seriously, recently a local bank was *not robbed* because the robber came after banking hours. Everyone got a good little laugh over that news report. The security video shows the would-be robber sneak up, catlike, to the Bank of America door, only to find it locked because it was after banking hours. The bank was closed; his plan was dashed. He pulled on the handle and then had to quickly scurry off with his mask still on. I don't know if the police were able to find him, and I'm not sure if he was arrested, but he had not robbed the bank, after all! Can you be arrested for trying to open the bank door after hours with a mask on? Either his negative angels he had attracted and created had really failed him and his sense of timing, or his personal guardian angel (who knew this wasn't his best option) may have done him a favor. Perhaps it was out of character for this guy to attempt a holdup; maybe he unconsciously saved himself as well, aligning with a higher presence within himself. If he was desperate and chose to try bank robbing in a moment of despair, his personal angelic protector was ever so glad. If the guy has not collected many negative angels (because he does not attract enough negativity to be skilled at this kind of sneaking thing) then his negative inclination was weaker than his positive inclination. Something about it made me think his angel of pure love knew how to get him to the bank after hours. Cosmic forces were not supporting his evil plan. Some might say he just wasn't very smart, but something tells me he inwardly didn't want to do it that badly. His guardian angel blocked it from happening.

So the angels are very patient with us, but let's think of all the great things that will flow our way when we do follow the quiet inner voice of the in-dwelling spirit, the guiding angel. There are so many wonderful, magical surprises that angels can give us when we tune in toward what is love-filled rather than slide around in the swamp of shadows. And even if we are as balanced and whole and loving as we know to be, life will still at times toss us into despair. Just know your angel will be there for you, even if the job of keeping you out of trouble is dreadful for them.

SOME WAYS TO GIVE YOUR ANGEL A BREAK

I share this working list, a work in progress, in the spirit of human imperfection. It is not like I am so great at it that I can tell anyone from on high how to do it. I have learned the hard way, through life experiences and as an intuitive for many years entering into meditation and spiritual truth-seeking. You will no doubt have your own to add to this list:

- If what you're about to do doesn't feel right, do not do it.
- Be open and ready to hear a cosmic "No, do not do this."

- Be open and ready to hear a cosmic "Yes, it is safe to do this."
- Ask, "What can I do to make the world better?"
- Feel the sensation in your heart as your guide.
- Be in a state of appreciation for what is good.
- Don't focus so much on all the problems; focus more on the solutions.
- Do to others what you'd have them do to you (always!).
- Ask for forgiveness from those you've harmed or hurt.
- Forgive yourself.
- Enjoy yourself, especially in some creative action.
- Do a kind deed, once a day at least.
- Take care of your body as a wondrous tool for beautiful gestures.
- Be respectful of others and the environment.
- Don't resist change when it arrives.

During the times that we declare our misery over our circumstances, we'd help the angels best by not *resisting change*. Okay, some things need to be outwardly protested, and sometimes having the courage to protest may actually be our soul challenge toward fulfillment. And I'm not suggesting hanging around while someone uses you as an inflated Bozo the Clown punching bag. Do what you have to do to be safe and healthy! What I am saying is that we help the angels help us best when we take a look at our circumstances and, no matter how badly things may be going, we help our angels and ourselves when we simply accept what is happening. And then be quiet. And then wait and see. And then move out or move on. When we make our decisions after getting in touch with angelic guidance, everything works out easier. Quite often with no effort at all on our part.

In dramatic times, do what you feel called to do. But to inwardly or outwardly resist change that is upon you, or to hold on to what is inevitably shifting, or to try to force things to remain the way you want them to be, is to go against what might be the best angelic intervention you've ever experienced. The ego will grip and pride will scratch and claw at change, but angels will gently soothe us if we let them. Try not fighting and see if powers more mysterious and greater than your might can come through for you. It may not look the way you wanted it all to look, and you may be forced to endure uncomfortable times, but trust that you are not alone and that you have angelic advocates who will carefully tend to your needs throughout.

Like I said, what looks like the most god-awful situation at one point in time, can end up being your ticket to bliss: care of your own personal guardian angel. Usually upon the quaking shift that is knocking you off balance, the shock and torment of change, or injury to ego identity, days of grief with sense of loss, all of it—may well be a supreme golden plan for you especially designed by your angel. But if you continue to fight, rip around angrily, resist the change, and curse the idiots who are putting you through it, you are not helping the angels help you.

If you have fear or anger, let yourself get it all out, but know all the while that as you gradually work through the hurt and anger, disappointment or fear, angels are sympathetic and feel your torment.

They do not want you to feel hurt. If you can surrender just a bit, even if it is only into your pillow sobbing at night, do it. The angelic love that surrounds you is not expecting perfection from you, but your cooperation with them, and accepting the turn of events may get you out of misery sooner than you imagined.

Guardian Angels Urge Forgiveness

Forgiveness plays a huge part in giving your angels a break. In an earlier chapter, we went over how forgiveness and empathy actually weave angelic gold for us. How can we forgive someone who got us fired, stole from us, took someone or something we love away from us, destroyed our way of life, or betrayed us? If we see them the way the angels see them, another sensation emerges, and it is mercy for the perpetrator. It may well be that the angels are working through the perpetrators to set you free. You've heard the saying, "What human-kind uses for evil, God uses for good." Evil exists, and we do not have to tolerate it or condone it and should do what we can to stop it, with angelic assistance. But not forgiving can cause us suffering (which can be another form of evil) and creates loss and spiritual dehydration.

The perpetrators creating victimhood in you may, without their knowing it, through their negative traits and choices, be breaking your life open so that you can live to the fullest. Angels may witness the crimes and put an equal amount of love in its place in ways that should become evident, whether through us or others or by unexpected outcomes. Consider it every time you face adversity. Stop and ponder—is an angel at work here for me? And if you ask, it will make it even more so an angelic life experience.

Not to forget that, at times, *we* are perpetrators to someone else—would we hope for mercy so that we could be forgiven for ways we may have injured someone?

We can make the job of our angels easier if we:

- Notice them working in our lives through our appreciation of nature and others in our midst.

- Take their presence and advice seriously but also with mirthful hearts (have a sense of humor!).

- Spend time and energy purposely developing our creative, intuitive intelligence and empathy (acts of kindness and care).

Remember these ways in which angels send us clues and cues:

- Synchronistic events, small and large. For example, I was texting a friend while a movie was on. I texted the word *plenty* at the exact moment it was said by a character in the movie, and a few seconds later I texted the word *forever* also at the exact same time the same character in the movie said *forever*! I do not know all that this may signify. I just know that I experience a steady flow of coincidental events that happen when I am in a good, open, and honest place with myself. I feel a bright feeling of harmony when these things happen.

- Journal dreams so that angel messages can be recorded, pondered, acknowledged—read and reread.

Guardian Angel Showed Me the Key

Just today I told a massage therapist about a dream I had last night where I was with a person I know and that person's angel showed up *in his place*. In other words, at one moment in the dream, he became his own guardian angel! And the guardian angel is one I had seen before in relation to this person. She's tall and has blondish hair, and she is very calm, kind, and virtuous. In the dream she showed me a heart locket she wanted, and it rested upon the heart when you put it on, but you could take it apart and there would be a key inside it.

When I woke up, I felt the message was that the "key to love" is to listen to and pay attention to the heart, the compelling inward voice that directs us to love rather than to obey our ego. Then, surprisingly, the massage therapist told me that she receives a daily message via text (with an app) and that her message of the day was eerily connected to the angel message I'd had in the dream a few hours earlier. She said, "The message for today was, 'Never give anyone else the key to your heart's happiness.'" She felt it meant that we ourselves are in charge of our happiness, not someone else, and that if we hand someone else the key to our happiness, we can easily blame them when we are not happy. Yet this is our own responsibility—we have to create and keep our own happiness.

That was a double message from that one angel, both in my own dream and in the therapist's daily message. A synchronistic sign showed me that an angel needed me to receive this very important message about the truths of the heart. I paid attention to the synchronicity and wrote it all down in my journal so that I would pay attention to the message more deeply.

ANGEL HINTS

As you allow angelic focus to be important to your day, you will start to see that the light in others' eyes is evidence of love. They may not be aware of this, but if you can see the flicker of soul-light in them, you will have made a very important connection on the deepest level—a connection that, when you behold it, frees you from absence of love.

This love comes through in many wonderful ways. Angels give us hints letting us know to tune in and experience this kind of magic. Nothing is ordinary once you've agreed to dance with angels and invite this abundant love into your being. Watching for the signs will make even the most mundane chores seem magical.

An owl hoots during the day and night right outside my window. One day as I walked my dog, I looked up to the treetops and said in a whisper, "Owl, I'd like to see you!" Within a week, I was amazed to find myself sitting a few feet from this owl! After hearing his call, I quietly sat on a rock to scan the trees in hopes of getting a glimpse of him. I did not have to strain to see him; he was simply enormous and majestic on a branch a few feet from me. For quite some time we sat staring into each other's eyes. I remained as still as possible. Eventually he began turning his head, returning to thoughts of hunting. And then he flew off, his silent wings wide and beautiful.

I was so taken by this rare gift that I walked my dog later that day and said, in a whisper, looking up at the trees, "Owl, thank you for visiting me. I loved having you visit me. Could you please let me have one of your feathers as a token of our connection?"

Then about a week later, I felt an angel hint! I allowed that hint to sway me. There on the ground near a tree was a magnificent owl feather! Would I have found the feather had I ignored the gentle hint?

These angelic whispers are always positive and never negative. They infuse us with a love that is ever-present, but we have to build our awareness and bond with angels. When we do, the thrill of such "wishes come true" makes life so rich.

ANGEL FACT: In most cultures, angels can fly and are able to arrive anywhere in the timing of their choosing. Their wings take on deeply symbolic meaning for humans. Wings signify the human ability to embody angelic ways through love, compassion, imagination, "flights of fancy," or creative, spiritual visualization.

9

communicate with your angels

When we communicate with others, angels are present. It is as if we are communicating to them. Given the way we communicate through social media, what kind of angelic energy are we tapping out of our fingers through the keyboard, sending out to the world? Every time we tweet or e-mail or text or type out thoughts on Facebook or other social media sites, know that we are whipping up a mighty flow of energy. Angels are summoned by our words and actions.

To counterbalance all we do in a given day in the way of communicating, interacting with others, and in our life choices, we dream. This is so we may have a chance to learn through our own unconscious as well as through spiritual, astral experiences. We learn to become more aware of ourselves, what we are saying and doing, what hurts us and what we desire, through dreams. Dreamscapes are the terrain of angels, and they will speak to us just like we speak to others with our devices these days—in angel time: in the blink of an eye. Massive amounts of angelic energy get sent out, emotion is transferred from us to another, and back to us.

HOW TO TALK TO YOUR ANGELS

Angels can be reached and the relationship with them deepened by writing your thoughts, feelings, reactions, animal sightings, and other signs and dreams in a journal.

What if You Feel You Can't Remember Your Dreams?

If you can't remember your dreams, there may be several reasons why. One might be that according to what you're doing in your life, it may not be your purpose at this time to remember your dreams. It may be best that you sleep soundly and wake up to do all the things you've got to do the way you do it. Even if this is so, trust that your angelic guides will respond if you decide you want to remember your dreams.

Another reason why you may not recall your dreams could be that you haven't developed it as a discipline. And so this is like anything else, it can be learned, taught, and trained.

Some Ways to Remember Your Angelic Dreams

State out loud, with authority, that you will remember your dreams (do this for at least two weeks).

- Journal this same statement, "Today I told the angels that I WILL remember my dreams."

- Repeat this statement when you go to sleep at night.
- Tell the angels all the reasons why you would love to have them visit you in dreams.
- Keep a dream journal/notebook and pen/pencil by your bedside.
- When you wake up, remain relaxed—don't move—stay in your dream consciousness.
- Hold any feelings or thoughts of dreams that might still be with you as you awaken.
- Write down any fragments or dream sequences before getting fully up and awake.

Sometimes dreams are not inspiring, due to something you ate or if you're not feeling great. At least some dreams are not in any way pleasant or transformative. But write them down, paying very close attention to how you felt in the dream. Focus on the feelings as the more spiritually significant factor of your dreams, so that locating the angel message in it is done so less by some form of analyzing, and more so through emotive, empathic sensing. Feel in your heart and nervous system how the dream made you feel. Stay with it. Ask yourself, "Where else have I felt this same sensation?" In other words, some life circumstance may occur to you where you had the same feeling the dream presented.

Holding the feelings of the dream, see it again in your mind's eye. What was the lighting like? Was it low and dark or bright and colorful? Was it a good feeling, or a shabby one? Again, try to locate that feeling in some life experience you have had, by quietly allowing the dream feeling to stir in you again. Once you recognize where and when you've had that feeling in waking hours (at school, at home, in childhood, with a partner, etc.), the dream will begin to guide you. You can apply the dream imagery to the feelings and the experiences you've had that gave you those feelings. Maybe new ways of perceiving your feelings will be revealed, new truths and new consciousness. Your angels may be helping you resolve some emotions that claim your spirit in some way, some hurt or lack of worth or even sense of preciousness that needs healing. For example, let's say you dreamed of a picnic by the sea with colleagues from work. But when you examine the feelings in the dream, you realize you've had that same type of feeling when your mother was unwell. You'd then apply the feelings about your mother's sickness to these people you work with (who were or are not at all connected in any way to your mother or the time she was unwell). Perhaps something about those colleagues or that work situation activates unconscious emotion from the point in time that your mother was unwell. Connections and realizations can be made and insights gained where you'd never normally even make the connections. Then this awareness can guide you.

FLY WITH ANGELS

It is really fun to cultivate dreams, to wish for them, journal your desire to have them, and meditate before falling asleep to visually create them. My favorite dream to create is flying dreams. I started to journal and visualize having a dream with light and joyous flying, but it took a few weeks of mental effort before my effort was rewarded. I'll share with you my experience, and you can try it using your own dream journal. Before falling asleep at night, I'd imagine as best I could how it might feel to rise up and float around the room from about three feet off the ground. This caused problems in my mind, as I imagined I'd hit my shins on table tops and bump into standing lamps, but that's okay, because you want the meditation to feel as "real" as possible. With nightly practice, this worked well. I gradually added to it; I'd imagine flying straight through the ceiling and roof or out the window. I would soar and dip all over town under a star-lit sky.

ANGEL FACT: *Zoroastrian* (ancient Persian) angels were assigned as guardians for every individual human being and were known as *fravashi*.

10

angel signs and synchronistic events

The angels are constantly trying to let us know they are right here with us. We have to want to engage with them if we want to really get to know them and see the ways they work their magic. Often enough we are simply, utterly lucky to have had some divine intervention. The angels will help us whether we realize it or not, but life is way more interesting when we not only believe in angels, but seek them and seek to understand their ways.

You can tell by obvious signs that your angels are with you, and these signs will indicate the essence or proclivity of the angel. It may be an angel to align you with creativity, or one to guide you toward common sense, or one that works to connect you to meaningful study. The angel you need will be with you.

SEEING VISIONS OF ANGELS

Synchronistic happenings abound when you are aligned with your angels. It is as if you are floating along a river, and everything is connected in a pleasant way. The sense of discourse or disease is gone. The smallest kind of synchronistic event matters when you're in touch with angels. The clock may display your lucky number when you look at it (mine is 3:33 and I'm always surprised when I glance over and it happens to be exactly 3:33!) or you think of someone at the moment right before they call you, these are in-sync experiences that bring delight and surprise because they're random, yet harmoniously presented. They're often called "coincidences"—but they're more.

Some Synchronistic Signs

- Your favorite number pops up either on a clock or other places.
- The person you just thought or spoke of calls you at that moment.
- Your favorite animal in the wild darts nearby.
- What you dreamed shows up in waking life.
- You say a word, then turn on the TV, and a character says the same word.
- You want something and, out of the blue, someone offers it to you.
- You ask a question in your mind and, not long after, someone answers the exact question (as if they—or your angels? —heard your inner mind).

Small Synchronistic Messages Pack a Punch

Yesterday, I was missing one of my favorite actors, Gene Wilder. I started to think of him and asked for a sign from the angels that somehow he'd know he was very appreciated by me. Silly, perhaps, but I asked. I also decided to read about him a little on the internet. I saw that he had a small role in the movie *Bonnie and Clyde*, one of his first acting roles in a major film. I don't like the story of Bonnie and Clyde or movies about them but liked that Wilder was in it and thought I'd like to see his part. Later that day, after working, I made a salad and turned the TV on to Turner Classic Movies. I saw that, lo and behold, *Bonnie and Clyde* was coming on soon. Now that was strange, I had only just read about it earlier in the day! Since I don't like the movie, I changed channels.

But some time later, I happened to flip through channels again when I passed by the TCM channel. What did I see right in the middle of the screen? Gene Wilder! I had turned the TV on to the exact one and only scene I'd want to see! I watched it for a few minutes until his role was over. And then I turned it off.

I did marvel at this little wish I had coming true very quickly! In one day, I asked the angels to show me a sign, and all the timing and the happenstance delivered it. That is the kind of synchronistic stuff angels are made of, and generously give us!

How to See Signs from Your Angels

- Notice hunches you receive.
- Watch for obvious signs of synchronicity in small and large ways.
- Notice animals that cross your path, especially any unusual sightings.
- Pay attention to inner feelings that warn you away from places or people.
- Pay attention to inner feelings that draw you toward places or people.
- Notice ways in which things happen that seem unlikely.
- Practice "spiritual seeing" with your third eye only (by closing your eyes during the day).
- Practice "gazing," looking at things spiritually with an open heart.
- Journal what comes to you in the way of signs and dreams.
- Watch for feathers, coins, or other small objects.

Minimovies

In addition, pay close attention to flashback memories you get of scenes of your life—angels will show us our actions through movie-like scenes. You may feel you have suddenly been sent back to a moment you forgot about long ago, or to a place that made a big impression on you. When you see scenes of your past interactions with others, there may be messages in them, messages of soul-awareness. Are you the same as you used to be? Did you say or do things you would not say or do today? Do you see why you acted or reacted the way you did? These are minimovies that show us our own personal soul records, known as Akashic records. Each thing we have said, thought, or done gets recorded in our soul records. Since we come into this life to learn, our angels want us to review and understand our growth, how far we have come or how far we still need to go, and do so with forgiveness of others and self. These minimovies help with that tremendously.

ANGEL FACT: There are angels in the Sikh religion called Chitar and Gupat who keep the soul records—every thought (conscious and unconscious), word, and action—of each individual.

11

astral energies: angels as abstract forms of color and light

Before reading this section of the book, try practicing the spiritual art of aura gazing. Start teaching yourself to see the luminous glow of color and light, which surrounds all things. The easiest way is to use contrast. Place a brightly colored orange, for example, on a blue surface, tablecloth, or painted surface. Orange and blue are opposites on the color wheel and this contrast will help you find the light that you normally may not be noticing. You can try it with a red apple against a green surface, or a yellow lemon against a purple surface. Or any solid color object against a white or gray surface. Once you have placed a solid colored object upon a surface with nothing else in view, you will relax and stare with soft eyes at the main object. As you stare in a relaxed way (this is called *gazing*) you may begin to see the thin line of color around the object. It is like an outline of light around the object. If you don't see it at first, keep practicing but remember you're doing this as a form of meditation, and you need to be very relaxed, very peaceful, as though you are in a daydream. If you like, have a person stand against a white or gray wall and gaze at them. You will begin to see the glow of light and color around them. Try it often, while at work or school. Go into your own inner space for a few minutes and let your spiritual way of perceiving get some of your time and attention.

Angelic messengers are not physical beings, but can assume physical form as needed. We, too, animate a body, but our consciousness is pure soul energy, held in the body while we are alive, for the most part. Some of our soul energy is always with the Great Creator. And a larger part of our consciousness can leave the physical body, especially during sleep.

ANGELS ARE ASTRAL (AND SO ARE YOU)

Every night when we sleep, we astrally travel (we go places in our dreams, where we experience and learn). What part of us is doing this undeniable excursion? If your actual body is in bed, how is your consciousness having a conversation with someone in China or with a friend you knew in high school or whatever the dream has you experiencing? We say it is the brain sloughing off our psycho-emotional collective stored in our unconscious. And it is all that, too, yet dreams cannot be denied and are more than that. Dreams are the astral playscapes where we can experience deep and real transcendence, serious and life-altering transformations of thought and feeling. The same transformational astral seeing can be experienced through medita-tion, and effortlessly when we receive flashbacks, which place us somewhere else suddenly in our mind's eye (or astral eye, third eye).

This soul energy that transcends corporeal, temporal matter (the body) is energy that is seen as undulating light and color, a "spark" in the great cosmos, a spark which is part of the One Great Light, Adonai, Source, Supreme Being, God, Great Spirit. That light and color is visually how angels may show themselves. Sometimes they may appear as a hologram, a body outlined in color and light, or as though solid and "real," yet shimmering or glistening in light, realer than real.

STARRY ANGELS

Often, in meditation, simply through closing my eyes, I see I am flying at warp speed through stars, or are they flying through me? Each pinpoint of light, millions of them, is possibly a soul traveling. I must also appear to them as a star, as a body of light. Are these stars angels or other human souls? There is so much mystery, I can only say the feeling of seeing them fly through me, or me through them, is perfectly blissful.

Angelic presences are often seen and comprehended in their pure light form, as a perceivable mass of soul consciousness. It is important to note that communication with angels, whether they're assuming the shape of another human being or animal, or whether they're in their abstract pure soul energy form, is mainly telepathic. You feel it in your heart, your entire being absorbs the information. If an angel needs to appear as a human and speak to you directly, he or she will and does, but otherwise, what they mean to convey, they do via their very presence, whether visible to us or not. To behold an angelic, astral, abstract form of luminous, pearlescent colors and light is pure ecstasy. The feeling transmitted is like a rush of unconditional love.

It Only Took One Look from My Angel

I had a flash of angelic, astral communication once. I was nearing a transition but was slow to move on. I was dating someone in medical school. He was studying while I was lying down resting. I saw in my mind's eye/third eye (eyes closed, but not asleep) a beautiful woman in a library. She had on a forest green velvet gown and a golden wreath of leaves in her coppery blond hair. She looked into my eyes; her face was serene and her bearing formidable. In that one instant, I "heard" her—she telepathically communicated to me that it was time to "meet your destiny" or "fulfill your purpose." The seriousness with which she gave me this important message was severe, yet she was kind. I guess you could say she gave me a shove to seize my life and move toward what my heart was calling me to do. In a single moment, I knew that it was time to move on. I felt the gravity in the message. I understood the mission of my life and felt that if I ignored her (but I would not imagine that even possible!), I would be very off track in my life's purpose. Shortly after that vision, I moved to Boston. The angel did not appear as an abstract form of color and light, rather as a 1500s kind of European muse, really. Yet the astral experience was the sudden visual flash that placed me in my angel muse's library so I could receive a message of the utmost importance.

And the same kind of message can be given when beholding an angel in pure radiant soul form, which in appearance is a lot like those wondrous Hubble space photos of galaxies, so stunning as to have hypnotic effect. Angels in their pure soul presence are shimmering light, abstract forms of color, a mass of intelligence and compassion blended—and these descriptive words I am using are inadequate. When I have seen such shimmering light and swirling color, I have felt the utmost bliss. (Besides the one time I felt the angel being's intelligence was so severely advanced, I almost cowered before it shot off and away.) Some are flying from left to right over the bed as I wake up, and the feeling then, too, is of excitement mixed with deep serenity.

Again, the angels in any form are a force of energetic consciousness, and humans in our animal state most certainly amuse them, as our own souls are dealing with base instincts and limitations of the physique. We gaze up at an angel, and our primitive instincts try to make sense of the moment, always with the impulse to survive. Are we dirty, funny, miraculous little packages of fraught material to these majestic presences?

WHEN CAN I SEE MY ANGELS?

The answer to this question is that we have no control over what, when, or how we come to see angels of any kind, yet the answer also is that we can cultivate, ask for, and receive visions of angels. Once we have a deeply held intention to learn more about angels, I personally believe through experience that we are shown as according to the will of God, in divine timing. Which means we may wait a long, long time, and usually it happens when we least expect it. You have to have a combination of deep desire and a sense of detachment around the idea for it to happen. You have to cultivate the desire, yet gently and loosely accept that it will come when it will. Any forced staring into space will not help, or bratty assertions (believe me, I've tried that!) while trying to meditate, nor pleading or begging. The best visions usually happen when you least expect them.

Gazing: How to See Your Angels

AURA GAZING: Have a person stand at a neutral-colored wall and relax your vision to see the glow of light around him/her.

GAZE FOR ORBS: Look at a blank ceiling while resting, relax your eyes to gaze mode, and allow your vision to soak up soft light and color.

GREEN MAN GAZING: While out in nature, see the faces in the trees and rocks.

The best time to see angels, I have found, is in the hypnogogic state, where you're falling asleep or you've slept and are awake, and relaxed enough to fall back to sleep, but you don't. You are not at all "on task" ("I've got to get up, do this, do that . . . etc." with your thoughts) and are still utterly and completely relaxed. Eyes are open softly. Between 3:00 A.M. and dawn, or any time you are able to meditate into that very relaxed, open state. For me, lying down flat works best, rather than in a yoga position. Your eyes are gazing—not seeing, but gazing. This is third-eye viewing with your physical eyes at service to the meditative level of awareness. Let your body stay in the deep sleep place of cloud-floating liquidity (like a ball of mercury rolling around). Or, if you're intentionally going to lie prone to rest and meditate this way to see if you can welcome angels, your body wants to feel that lightness of being as though you are ready to float or slide away. This is not to say that you can't spontaneously see an angel. You might be busy doing things and all of a sudden have a surprise visitor, seeing a shimmering, exquisite, and luminous orb above you.

I recommend getting very practiced at the art of gazing, opening to the idea of seeing auras and orbs especially. Orbs of light are very soothing to see, as are the other magnificent angel forms of light and color. They are, as my Cherokee mentor stated, very much like "babies," new souls observing us shyly. They tend to glide like large pearls to the corner of the room, behind you, once you spot them. The others are giving me a totally different feeling—like being confronted or examined by an all-knowing (or at least way more knowing than humans) celestial inhabitant.

GAZING AT AURAS

You can experiment with light and the qualities and frequencies of light that give us the perception of color. Look at a color wheel and get ready to angel-play with complementary colors. You'll see on the wheel that there are both primary and secondary colors. Primary colors are red, yellow, and blue. Secondary colors are orange (between red and yellow), green (between yellow and blue), and purple (between blue and red). Every color is complementary to the color across from it on the wheel. For example, look at orange and note that it is directly across from blue. The tones and values of the secondary colors will vary, and you'll want to match the variation as best you can in any two objects.

Find a blue tablecloth or large piece of paper. The blue should be as primary a blue as you can find. Put the blue cloth on a table and then place a large, bright-orange object on the blue cloth. Sit down nearby and prepare to gaze.

Allow your eyes to relax. As you focus on the orange, be aware of your peripheral vision. As you gaze this way, easing gently into allowing your sight to become a meditation tool, you'll start to see the light that encircles the contour of that bright orange on the blue tablecloth. That light you'll see is the aura of the object. It will have a vibrancy that is potent and electric-looking. You may notice what color it is. It may have bands of color in it as you deepen your gaze. This works best if you stare in a relaxed way at the center of the orange.

Another exercise for seeing the energy of angels through light and color is gazing when you're in the bathtub! Lay back, relax in the water, and stare at your foot as it rests against the other end of the tub. Either foot will do. Gaze meditatively at the foot and continue until you feel you're in a trance. As you do this, you'll begin to see the outline of brilliant light contouring your foot. What color is it? The color you see is the essence color of your aura. Mine is an aqua blue-green. Sometimes it is more green than blue, other times more blue than green.

Enjoy your vision experiments as they lull you and love you into angel-sight!

ANGEL FACT: Angel's Landing is an ancient, dramatic rock formation, one of the many stunning peaks in Zion National Park in Utah. There is a path cut into the rock and tourists climb it to the summit. It was named Angel's Landing after someone commented that only an angel could land on top of it.

12
stories of angel sightings

I had a period of time in my twenties when, after ending a bad romantic relationship, I longed for a better one. I never quite met the right person, though, and so there were a few years where I felt deep sorrow and lack. I had been to Ireland and was given a claddagh ring. It is a ring made of silver depicting two hands holding a heart. The shop person told me, "If you're taken, you wear the ring with the point of the heart facing your heart." She continued, "But if you're not taken yet, you wear the ring facing outward so everyone knows you are not yet taken." I immediately put the ring on facing outward, as if to say, "Hello, everyone! I'm available!"

I wore this ring constantly, which means rather than just living and being happy, I was always reminded of the thought, "I'm not taken. I'm not in a romantic relationship," and it was a sad way to be. After a few years of this, I had a dream that changed it all. In the dream, it was a very sunny country day. I stepped up to a dirt road and looked left, then right. I saw two people far down the road talking and walking toward me. I felt so good in the dream, the sun was warm and the day was bright. As the two walkers got closer to me, I saw that one was a young man and the other was an older man, wearing a headdress. This looked to be a big frog headdress. He also wore a robe, while the young man wore contemporary clothes like a shirt and jeans. In the dream I said to myself, "Oh, he is a frog shaman." As they walked and gestured during their conversation, I watched them. And as they passed by me, the frog shaman turned to me and said, "Take off that ring and never wear it again!" And he kept walking.

When I woke up, I took off the ring and flung it across the room. I realized this was an angel schooling me on energy work of the most essential kind, what was termed "law of attraction." Basically, what you put out, you get back. Okay, so I had thought I was telling the world, "Hey, I'm single! I want a mate!" When in fact what I was sending out was more like this message: "Well, I'm alone. And here's my ring to prove it. As you can see I am very lonely. I don't have anyone to love." And *that* was the lesson—to realize that what I was sending out energy-wise was a message I did not intend. And the universe was giving me back what I had sent out—a feeling of lack thereof when it came to boyfriends. After I stopped wearing the ring and stopped focusing on what I didn't have and tried to connect more to the feeling of general happiness and "Aren't boyfriends great to have?" and that enthusiasm was better energy for getting a boyfriend than the sorrowful "I don't have a boyfriend" vibe I had been cultivating, with the ring galvanizing my feeling of loss. And so it was not too long after tossing that ring as my frog shaman angel had ordered (and that he did!), that I met someone, and within a few years we were engaged and married.

CHIEF OSCEOLA ANGEL

I want to tell you about the most powerful visitation I had of an angel, within a dream and in real waking time. It clearly shows how angels can work through us and others in concert, to impact our practical lives and our relationship to the Source of Life. It also illustrates how our human longing, angst, and prayers are heard and answered with mighty reinforcements that confound humans attempting explanations.

I was in my early twenties and in dire circumstances, in a relationship that essentially was not safe. Yet I did not know how to navigate myself beyond and away from this terrible situation. So, I started to feel entirely lost and afraid, weak and incapable of escaping it. I thought of my grandfather who had died when I was about fifteen. He was a very strong and formidable man, I knew he would not have allowed me to get myself into such a situation so I prayed for him to help me. At that time, I was also learning a lot about Native American spirituality and liked the term "Grandfather Spirit." So, in my prayers, I combined my love of my grandfather with my desire to be spiritually rectified and continually asked "Grandfather Spirit" to please help me.

As I prayed all the time in my mind, no matter what I was doing, I also prayed for an ideal job, that of artist-in-residence at a local public school. I had worked for the local museum for years and as an art teacher in summer camps, and it was time to progress. So I prayed for an artist-in-residence position somewhere. Things felt worse by the day, but I kept praying. I had never felt more powerless.

Then one night I had a dream that the apartment I lived in with the person who was so toxic for me was on fire. In the dream, I ran to the door, but I could not open it. There appeared at the door a very handsome man, a Native American. He wore a white turban on his head with a feather in it and buckskin. He said to me, "Elaine. Open. The. Door." He was very authoritative. I answered him, "Look, I can't open it; it's locked." I pointed to the several large bolt locks on the door. The Native American man repeated, "Elaine, open the door!" This time, he said it a little louder. Again, I said, "I can't open it; it's locked!"

And then in a raised, very stern voice, he said, "Elaine, GO THROUGH THE DOOR!" I did exactly as he said, I started to move through the actual door. I saw the fine details and grooves in the grain of the wood as I passed through! I found myself on the other side of the door—I was free! And the Native American man was right there with me. I was thrilled; I was saved! He had helped me get out. I loved him eternally for it. He began to back up into the woods, saying with each step back, staring at me in the eyes, "I'm still here. I'm still with you." And he disappeared into the trees.

When I woke up from this dream, I was shocked by its powerful scenario and how free I felt—I had a new power within me. I started to feel very different, no longer weak, but with a new plan to finally break through and make a life change. The unrelenting sureness that this Native American hero of mine had was in me and with me still. I now *had* to "go through the door," literally and figuratively. But as the days went by, for some reason, I discounted that this hugely impressive dream was "real." I started to tell myself that it was only psychologically symbolic, and anyway, my mind had confused Native Americans with people from India because, after all, Native Americans did not wear turbans, but people from India did. So this incredibly austere angel who loved me tremendously and forced me to muster up strength, I told myself, didn't exist.

Then I got a phone call. It was the art center calling and asking me to work as an art teacher for summer camp again. I declined, explaining that I didn't want to do that anymore; I had done that job far too long and it was time to do a new job. He listened to me as I said no to him and then he said, "Well, if you do this summer camp job, I'll give you an *artist-in-residence* job at a local public elementary school." I was shocked! It was the exact job I had been praying for! I said yes. And when I showed up to teach, with pride, as the school's artist-in-residence, guess what the one who hired me said to me? He smiled and said, "And you, Elaine, will be teaching Native American arts." I could not believe it. Things were falling into place in the most surprising ways, as if my prayers were heard.

Then another thing happened. A friend told me she'd like me to come visit a private school with her, that she wanted to apply to teach there. I went along for the heck of it. I did not have an interest in the school. But while there, someone handed my friend an application, and then they handed me one. My friend filled hers out, so I filled out mine, too. Later we talked with one of the teachers, an African American woman who I had a great rapport with while talking about the volunteer work I had done in the rural South and the job I had at one time helping teach children at a Cesar Chavez Migrant Camp. We left the school and I didn't think about it again, but within a week I was asked to come in and interview for a job with the teacher I had spoken with that day when my friend and I visited. I almost skipped going to the appointment. I had no interest in teaching at a private school, I assumed it would be elitist and not my kind of place. At the last moment, I decided to go. I was hired. And I was excited about it. I decided it was a positive and happy place and that I should accept the offer. It happened so fast!

On my first day teaching at this school, a head teacher handed me a large coffee table book and asked me to explore it with a small group of kids. I said, "Sure," and sat down with the kids on the floor. I opened the book. And there *he* was! Staring at me, in his most utterly beautiful native tribal clothes, was Chief Osceola. And, yes indeed, he wore a white turban, with a feather in it. I was in the best kind of shock you can imagine. It meant that my dream had been very real, that dismissing it was a mistake, and that this is the exact one who helped me escape in answer to my prayers! As I read to the children about Chief Osceola, I discovered more, and it all fit in unbelievable ways. Chief Osceola was from the Creek Tribe of Georgia (exactly where I was living at the time!) and that as Andrew Jackson chased the Creeks out of Georgia, Osceola became known as Chief of the Seminoles, the word *Seminole* meaning "Tribe without a home." Osceola fled with his tribe to Florida, where he eluded capture over and over. And when they imprisoned him, *he escaped*. Chief Osceola, my very own angelic hero, escaped prison. Just like he appeared before me and showed me how.

Not long after this experience, I did go through that door (with one suitcase in hand) and was forever changed. I had this great angel to thank, in the form of Chief Osceola. To add another sweet droplet to this amazing spiritual experience that changed my life, I found out that one of my ancestors, on my grandpa's side (the one I missed and admired for his strength of character) was Native American. Guess what tribe he belonged to? Creek.

ANGEL FACT: In Western Judaic culture, angels are not to be worshipped but rather invoked for guidance, assistance, and intercession.

ACKNOWLEDGMENTS

I'd like to thank my dad for always nurturing me spiritually. He always had the best spiritually themed books before anyone else even knew about them. A book that had a very big impact on me and my spiritual development was handed to me at about age fifteen, when my dad ran into me in the hallway at home and gave it to me, saying he thought I'd really like it. It was *Return from Tomorrow* by Dr. George Ritchie. Dr. Ritchie's book was his personal story of being pronounced dead and then being revived, the details of which are fascinating. It was Dr. Raymond Moody's first such case study of this phenomenon, called Near Death Experience or NDE (a term that Dr. Moody coined). I was so impressed with Dr. Ritchie and his experience that I dared to write him a fan letter. And he answered! So we exchanged a few letters, which also made an important impression on me. That he was kind enough to answer my letters meant so much to me, and I never forgot it.

Due to Dr. Ritchie's generosity, my spiritual path and interest in dreams and angels expanded and set me on a course for life.

Then, many, many years later, I began writing books on intuitive intelligence and needed a new literary agent—I had been a children's book author and artist for years, and spiritually themed books were a new genre for me. I remember fervently praying for things to fall in place so that the book I wanted to work on would find a home and get into the hands of those seeking to develop their empathic senses. Then one day an e-mail came to me from a stranger: author and therapist Dr. Laurie Nadel. She had read my first book on intuition, *Illuminara Intuitive Journal with Cards*, and wanted to tell me that she liked it. I was honored by her positive comments and thoughtfulness. I asked her if she had an agent who she could recommend, and she said yes. She gave me the name of Lisa Hagan, and we set up a phone conference.

By talking about all the books we grew up with that were major influencers, such as the writings of Edgar Cayce, Lisa and I discovered that we had a lot in common. When I told her about the book that had the most impact on me, *Return from Tomorrow* by Dr. George Ritchie, and that Dr. Ritchie and I had even exchanged letters, there was a pause before Lisa responded. She said, "Elaine, I grew up with Dr. Ritchie. I've known him all my life."

Lisa and I realized that some serious angel magic had taken place. How could it be that my love for a book, begun at age fifteen, had somehow connected me decades later (without my having to exert any effort, strain, or struggle) with an agent of spiritually themed books—an agent who had grown up with the author of that very same book? It could only be attributed to angels!

Lisa and I have remained very connected and have worked together ever since. Nobody will ever get me to agree that anything other than angels were at work in introducing us. The angels who guide us all are who put us together, effortlessly. I could not have made any of that happen had I tried. As we each focus on fulfilling our individual purpose and align with our truest ideals,

I think the angels have such fun swooping in with great surprises like this one.

And so, it is with deep gratitude that I thank God and the angels for prayers answered and that I thank my father for giving me Dr. Ritchie's book at age fifteen. I thank Dr. Nadel for supporting me as a new author in the mind-body-spirit genre years ago. And lastly I want to thank Lisa Hagan of Lisa Hagan Literary for enriching my life so beautifully through our books and through showing me that angels are present, always.

ABOUT THE AUTHOR

Elaine Clayton is an author, artist, Reiki Master, and intuitive reader. She writes and illustrates books for children, including books by Pulitzer Prize–winning author Jane Smiley and by Gregory Maguire, author of *Wicked*, which was adapted into the popular Broadway musical of the same name. She has two sons, Jonah and Alistair, and lives in Connecticut.

INDEX